ARTIFICIAL INTELLIGENCE AND DESIGN

INNOVATIONS AND INSIGHTS

Rahat K Dutta

HOW
ACADEMICS
an imprint of Highlyy Publishing LLP

ISBN: 978-93-6009-170-5
First Published : 2025

Published by : HOW ACADEMICS
an imprint of Highlyy Publishing LLP

Correspondence Address : 4/30 A II Floor, Double Storey Buildings
Vijay Nagar, Delhi-110009
Editorial: +91 9811026449
Sales : +91 9999953412
Email: info@howacademics.com
Website: www.howacademics.com

Printed in India

Contents

List of Figures

List of Tables

Preface

In recent years, the fusion of artificial intelligence (AI) and design has sparked a revolution, reshaping industries and challenging our understanding of creativity. "Artificial Intelligence and Design – Innovations and Insights" emerges from this dynamic intersection, offering readers a comprehensive exploration of how AI is transforming the design landscape and pushing the boundaries of what is possible. The inspiration for this book stems from my deep fascination with both technology and the creative process. As a designer and technologist, I have witnessed firsthand the incredible potential of AI to enhance, accelerate, and even redefine design practices. However, with this potential comes a host of new questions and challenges: What does it mean for a machine to create? How can AI augment human creativity without overshadowing it? And how can we ensure that these powerful tools are used ethically and inclusively in the design world? This book is an attempt to answer these questions and more. It is structured to provide both a broad overview and in-depth insights into the role of AI in design and UI. We begin with a historical perspective, tracing the evolution of design from traditional methods to the digital age, leading to the emergence of AI as a creative partner. Understanding this context is crucial to appreciating the significance of the current AI-driven innovations in design. The book explores specific areas where AI is making a profound impact. From generative design, where algorithms produce thousands of design variations in minutes, to AI-driven user experience (UX) optimization, the book showcases cutting-edge technologies that are revolutionizing design practices across industries. Through case studies and real-world examples, we highlight how companies and designers are leveraging AI to create more efficient, personalized, and innovative solutions.

However, this book is not just about technology; it is also about the human element in design. We look into the ethical considerations and potential pitfalls of AI in design, addressing concerns such as algorithmic bias, intellectual property, and the displacement of traditional design roles. I believe that as we embrace AI, we must also be mindful of its limitations and the need to maintain a human-centered approach to design. Another key focus of this book is the collaboration between human designers and AI. Far from replacing human creativity, AI offers a new set of tools that can inspire, challenge, and elevate the work of designers. We explore how this collaboration can lead to innovative outcomes, where the strengths of both human intuition and machine precision are harnessed to create groundbreaking designs.

This book is intended for designers, technologists, business leaders, and anyone interested in the evolving relationship between AI and creativity. Whether you are a seasoned professional or a curious newcomer, I invite you to explore the innovations and insights presented in these pages. Together, we can navigate the exciting challenges and opportunities that lie ahead as we shape the future of design with AI.

Chapter 1
Designing in an AI-Enhanced World

Introduction

A lot of attention and focus has been paid to the use of artificial intelligence (AI) in almost every industry, from making cars to providing healthcare. AI is changing our economy and ushering in a new era of industrialization. It is working with digital devices, networks, and software-based automation to make these changes possible. From Alibaba to Airbnb, a new type of company with a "digital" business model has come into being in this new "Age of AI," which has brought both new possibilities and challenges.

As companies move toward an operating model that relies more on AI, they are digitizing more and more important business processes. This takes away the need for human labor and management in many critical running activities. In contrast to how things work in regular businesses, no one sets the price of an Amazon item or decides if a business can get a loan from Ant Financial's bank. While people came up with the algorithms and wrote the software code, digital technology makes it possible for the answer to be made automatically and in real time.

As the market changes, so does the way things are designed. Sensors, digital networks, and algorithms are being used more and more. Whether our product is entirely software, like an iPhone app, or more traditionally hardware-based, like a Tesla car, modern products are becoming more and more connected to the company that made them, providing a constant flow of data that describes many aspects of the use experience. Additionally, the software built into the goods lets information flow from the designer to the user, so that a custom solution can be made for each user and the experience is always getting better in real time. These instant, two-way feedback loops are now found in more and more goods and services, from Netflix to the Tesla Model 3. In a way, these goods' designs change as the user interacts with them.

Because of this, AI could completely change the way planning is done. What does this mean for the way we practice design and how we think about creativity that is driven by design? This chapter looks at how AI is changing design by looking at the strategies of companies like Netflix and Airbnb that are at the cutting edge of where AI and design thought meet.

Our analysis addresses three questions:

- AI and the practice of design: to which extent AI is likely to change the way design is practiced? Is the transformation of the context induced by AI changing the design process and the objects of the design actions?
- AI and the principles of design: if so (i.e. if AI induces significant changes in the design practice), are these changes so deep to question the fundaments of design, such as, for example, user centeredness? Is design practice, in the age of AI, informed by significantly different principles?
- the theory of design: what are the implications for the theoretical frameworks that we use to interpret design? Does the age of AI call for new research questions and for a new understanding of how design drives innovation in organizations?

This is how the group is organized. First, we'll talk about what design is and how it works, which will help us answer the first two points. The ideas come from the theory of design thought that already exists. There is a structure that is used to compare the nature of design that relies on humans and design in the age of AI. Then, two examples of Netflix and Airbnb are used to show how the system works in real life. After that, we talk about the cases (with help from extra knowledge from Tesla and Microsoft's experiences) to figure out how AI changes design principles and practice. Finally, we look at what this means for design ideas and what designers do now in companies that use AI.

Exploring the Operating Context of Design

We will talk about AI and design on two levels: practice and ideas. This will help us figure out if and how much AI changes the way we think about design. The design practice is the experience of design in a certain setting. It includes the process (the "how of design" or things like stages, methods, tools, or working together) and the result of design (the things it makes). The design principles are the ideas and ways of thinking that guide the process of creating and make up an ontology of what design is. The difference between these two types of analysis helps us figure out what kind of effects AI has on design. Is AI altering the way we design, or is it even going deeper by challenging the fundamental ideas that drive the act of designing? In order to answer this question, let's begin by talking about the design principles that come from the current discussion on design theory. Next, we'll show how these principles have been used in design practice before AI came along, and finally, we'll talk about a way to look at how these principles are used in the new setting of AI Factories.

Understanding Design Principles

In the end, to design means to "plan actions that will change current situations into desired ones." To design means to come up with ideas that are more meaningful to people in order to move toward preferred situations. What are the ideas that guide this way of designing? There have been a lot of important additions to the scientific debate on the ontology of design in the field of design theories. Because we are interested in design methods in business settings, we use the newest findings from a certain field of research: design thinking. Even though the word "design" can mean more than one thing, management scholars who have tried to boil down the design principles that apply to organizations have come up with three main principles:

- **People-centered**: innovation, when driven by design, is inspired by empathy with users. Rather than being driven by the advancements of technology and by what is possible, design-driven innovation stems from understanding a problem from the user perspective, and from making predictions about what could be meaningful to her. For example, we can recognize this principle in the practice of ethnographic research.
- **Abductive**. design has a generative approach to create solutions. Rather than leveraging solely on deductive reasoning (how things are) and inductive reasoning (how things likely are), design creates through abductive reasoning, i.e. by making hypotheses about how things might be. Abductions often lead to reframing the problem and the question that informs the design. For example, we can recognize this principle in the practice of brainstorming.
- **Iterative**: abductions are continuously adapted and improved through fast testing cycles. Prototypes act as "playground" for conversation and learning. They engage the team and the users, enable to communicate ideas, fail, learn, and drive progress until a satisfying solution is achieved. For example, we can recognize this principle in the practice of building rudimental mockups early in the design process.

Navigating Design in Traditional Operating Models

The way these design concepts are used in real life depends on the situation in which the design is being done. Most of the design methods we use today were created in settings that depend on work and management. In order to create a new product, complex process architectures had to be made so that the product could be delivered at a large scale. Due to the large size of this organization, traditional companies released new goods in batches, and there were cycles of design (coming up with a useful solution), make (producing and marketing that solution on a large scale), and use by customers (see Figure 1). Different goods and services were made for "segments" of users, with customization options during production, because it wasn't possible or cost-effective to make a solution that worked for every single user.

The situation changed after a product came out. The market might have changed, or new technological possibilities might have come up. The way people actually used the current product could also teach designers new things. But because redesigning a product required a lot of work and money, new ideas were put on hold until the market value of a new product was higher than the cost of designing it. This was the start of a new design period.

Figure 1. Design practice in the context of traditional human-intense operating models

So, this kind of arrangement meant that there would be a big gap in time between two subsequent design projects. During this time, learning processes stopped moving forward, so answers quickly became "old." It was only possible to use new information and ideas in future products that came out in chunks, episodes, and for specific groups of customers.

Design in the context of AI Factories

Design work has traditionally been done by humans, but AI has the potential to change this. First, AI Factories can use real-time data from interactions with customers or data from the ecosystem in which the company operates to help the planning process. Even more interestingly, these data can also be used to teach AI systems things. And these engines can solve problems: if they are designed correctly, they can come up with specific answers for each user without any help from a person. Next, we'll talk about how this new scenario works using examples from Netflix and AirBnB, two companies that are at the forefront of using AI in design. Before we get into the examples of the cases, we'd like to show you a structure that helps us better understand the new ways that those companies have changed the way they do design (see Figure 2).

Figure 2. Design practice in the context of AI Factories

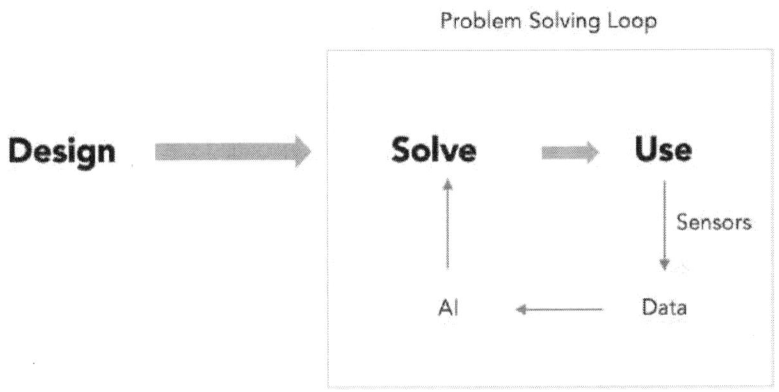

To create something means to make a choice. A few of them are very complicated and need a lot of thought and creativity. Most choices, especially those made early in life, need more specific problem-solving skills than creativity, though. These are decisions like what information to show on a screen, what shape an item should have for its purpose, and how the product should be interfaced with by a user. During the planning process, there are many small issues that need to be dealt with. AI has the smarts to figure them out.

In the setting of AI factories, designers can get away from having to work on small details of development. An AI engine is in charge of creating a specific answer, which is what a user actually interacts with. This process is known as "problem solving loops." These loops gather information (insights) about a single user, mix them with other information, and feed them into an algorithm that creates the best solution for that user. The solution is created at the exact moment the user requires it. Also, as new data is constantly added and AI engines are built with learning features, the problem-solving loops get better at guessing what users want and how they will act, which leads to better solutions being created. That is, answers are always getting better and new ones are being made.

In this AI-era, designers' jobs aren't to come up with products that can be sold on a large scale. Instead, they have to come up with a new product or service and then design the problem-solving loops that will create and give the right solutions for each user. There are two major functions that make up the problem-solving loops. First, being able to use sensors to collect, clean, and normalize data and then add it to a company data lake. Second, the ability to solve a customer's problem: in this chapter, we'll be talking about AI engines, which are made up of rules, theories, programs, and algorithms that can do smart things like recognize objects, process natural language, make predictions, and come to conclusions. These engines also have the ability to learn (machine learning), which lets them provide better solutions over time.

As a result, problem-solving loops are self-sufficient and don't require human capital. Instead of people, they use computers to come up with a solution. They can handle changes in volume without having to redesign or upgrade their operating model, and they can come up with a wide range of solutions without a lot of research and development.

AI-Empowered Design in Practice

We looked at the examples of Netflix and AirBnB to see how the system in Figure 2 works in real life. We chose these two cases because they are on the cutting edge of AI uses and show how design will change in the future with AI Factories.

Netflix and the data-driven, design thinking machine

Using the power of big data and AI, Netflix has totally changed the way media is made. Netflix's data and AI-based working model is what makes the company work. It runs on software infrastructure that collects data, trains and runs algorithms that control almost every part of the business, from making the user experience more personalized to choosing which movie ideas will be made. This part goes into more depth about Netflix's design process by looking at some of the machine learning tools that Netflix has used in its problem-solving loops.

AI has been used by Netflix since at least 2010 to power its selection engine. In 2014, Netflix added to the factory so that they could learn more about how users behave and make sure that each user had a unique viewing experience. There is a machine that "designs in the moment" the app screens that users see today. At the start of the process, human designers set a lot of limits and guidelines. An AI problem-solving loop, on the other hand, makes choices about which movies to show, how to show them, what pictures to use to represent them, and many other design choices. Let's look more closely at these algorithms, which are a lot like different parts of the planning process.

Most AI systems try to solve simple problems that have to do with predicting what will happen. An algorithm, which is a set of rules that a computer follows to solve a problem, is what was used to make that guess. AI can use a lot of different kinds of algorithms for a lot of different tasks. Some of the most interesting algorithms have a way to update and make them better built right in. These are usually based on "Markov Decision Processes," which try to model a series of actions, each shaped by a policy and followed by an award. Such an example is Netflix's algorithms, which change the user interface based on what the user does, as shown by the clicks. The policy chooses what is shown, and the click is the "reward."

Even though the number of uses has grown a lot in the last ten years, the basics of designing algorithms have been around for a long time. Classical statistical models, such as linear regression, clustering, and Markov chains, have been thought up and worked out mathematically for more than one hundred years. Neural networks were first created in the 1960s, but they are only now being used on a large scale with results that are ready for production. Almost all of Netflix's production-ready and running AI systems use one of three main ways to use statistical models, also called machine learning, to make correct predictions. The three types are reinforcement learning, supervised learning, and uncontrolled learning.

Supervised Learning. When supervised machine-learning systems try to guess what will happen, their main goal is to get as close as possible to an expert (or a reliable source of information). The most common case is figuring out from a picture whether the subject is a cat or a dog. The expert in this case would be any person with good eyesight who could tell whether a picture was of a cat or a dog. To start supervised learning, you need to get or make a set of data that has been identified. After that, the data are split into two groups: training and confirmation. We can tell if we are happy with the error between the algorithmic model's prediction of the result and the labeled outcomes that have been checked and confirmed by experts. If we're not happy, we can go back and do things a different way using statistics, get more information, or try to find other factors that might help us make a better guess. Netflix uses supervised learning in a number of different situations. Netflix has used labeled data sets of actions and results (like movies chosen and liked) by people the computer thinks are like a certain user in order to make suggestions. It is possible to make good suggestions based on a large set of user choices that have been adjusted by the user and the decision situation.

Keep in mind that some parts of guided learning are like human design, which was shown earlier in the first principle of design (people-centeredness). As human designers get into the situation of use and pay attention to every part of the user experience, so do algorithms. They are taught by a stream of relevant user data that includes details about the situation of use, like the type of device used, the time and place of action, and so on. The problem-solving processes work better when there are more observations and more steps in the process.

Unsupervised Learning. Unsupervised learning algorithms are used to find insights in data without any assumptions or prior knowledge. This is different from supervised learning models, which teach a system to recognize known results. In supervised learning, each piece of data is labeled with a certain outcome. In unsupervised learning, on the other hand, algorithms try to find "natural" groupings in the data, without labels, and find structure that might not be clear to the human eye. If we use pictures of cats and dogs as an example, an unsupervised learning program could find more than one way to group them. These could separate pictures of cats and dogs, pictures taken inside and outside, pictures taken during the day or at night, or almost anything else, depending on how the groups are set up. This is when someone doesn't know exactly what to look for but is trying to find linked groups or events that do or do not fit well-known patterns. Netflix uses unsupervised learning to find groups of customers who watch the same things by analyzing watching data. This can be done to make customer segments for marketing campaigns or to make different versions of the user interface for users who use the service in different ways. Netflix goes even further by using data and AI algorithms to figure out what material to make before it even starts. The first time predictive analytics was used was in 2013, when Media Rights Capital and others looked at the possibilities of House of Cards. The new series was a big hit, and Netflix kept making new shows based on accurate predictions about the market and how people would use their accounts. VP of original content Cindy Holland said in an interview, "We have projection models that help us figure out how big an audience might be for a certain idea or area based on certain factors about it." We have a structure for themes that basically tells us where we have a lot of programs and where we have room for growth.

Keep in mind that unsupervised learning is not a planned process. The patterns that appear at the end are based only on the findings (the data) and were not planned at the start of the process. At its core, the algorithm mimics induction. However, when run over a very large amount of data, unsupervised learning generates insights and theories that are similar to human abductions or the way people come up with ideas and brainstorm. So, unsupervised learning also builds design thought into the AI factory's problem-solving loops.

Reinforcement Learning. The third type of machine learning is reinforcement learning, which is most like a standard design process in how it works. Some of the uses of reinforcement learning might be even bigger than those of controlled and unsupervised learning. In reinforcement learning, you only need a starting point and a performance function. In supervised learning, you start with data on how an expert sees the result. In unsupervised learning, you start with a pattern and anomaly recognition system. Starting in a certain place, the system looks into the area around it to see if it has made a performance better or worse. The main choice is whether to spend more time learning about the complicated world around us or to use the model we've already made to guide our choices and actions.

Let's say we take a cable car up a big mountain and then want to walk down. It's very foggy today, and there aren't any clear tracks on the mountain. As we look around, we have to find the best way down because we can't just see it. We have to choose between the time we spend walking around the mountain to get a feel for it and the time we spend walking down once we think we've found the best way to get there. This is what you give up when you choose between exploring and exploiting. We will be more sure that we know the best way down if we spend more time exploring. However, if we spend too much time exploring, we won't have time to use what we find and walk down.

In reality, this is pretty close to how Netflix's system customizes movie suggestions and the images that go with them. Netflix realized that its viewers have a huge range of tastes and interests by looking at their user data. In order to do this, it decided that each user should be shown a cover art piece made just for her from movie frames. The artwork would draw attention to the parts of the title that are important to that person. The problem was tricky because the Netflix team had to choose which movies to show and then decide which artwork to go with each movie to make the best match between user and suggestion. A typical TV show season has about 10 episodes, which adds up to almost 9 million frames. It would be tedious and pointless to ask creative editors to quickly look through that many frames of movies in order to create a piece of art that will grab people's attention. It would not be possible to make a piece of art that fits the tastes of every single user. However, AI Factories, and especially reinforcement learning loops, are a good way to solve this design issue. Netflix uses reinforcement learning (and specifically multi-arm bandit algorithms) to spend some time exploring possibilities and some time taking advantage of the solution its models offer. This is similar to the last example where we were trying to find our way down the mountain. Netflix randomly shows different visuals to each user so that they can see more choices and help improve the prediction model. Netflix then uses the better model to show a certain user a bunch of suggestions that look better. Netflix keeps getting better by switching between times of exploration and exploitation on its own. This is done to learn as much as possible about the tastes of a complex human being and keep this particular user interested over time.

Keep in mind that reinforcement learning is a lot like the process of human design in a lot of ways, especially the earlier concept of iterations. This is because it focuses on finding a balance between exploitation and exploration. Opening the funnel with broad exploration can lead to more interesting and creative choices, just like with traditional design methods. However, it can also be harder to make sure that the exploitation phase leads to a usable solution.

When Netflix first started out, twenty years ago, it made money by shipping DVDs. Netflix could only see which titles users watched, how long they kept a DVD, and how they ranked each title with this mail delivery service. They couldn't see how users actually watched DVDs. Even though Netflix knew it was important to use data to improve the customer experience, it was hard for it to design because its assets and processes were so heavy. But when Netflix launched its streaming service in 2007, the company used the chance to turn its business plan into an AI factory. With streaming, Netflix could keep track of the whole user experience, like what device people use to watch the shows and when they stop, rewind, or skip during a show. It was possible to create several problem-solving loops that take design principles to their utmost level: a design that is focused on the user for every single user. And even more, to keep coming up with new ways to help that particular person. With the goal of giving her the most meaningful state-of-the-art answer at any given time. Because Netflix has problem-solving loops, each user experience is made just for them at that very time. While he was in charge of communications at Netflix, Joris Evers said, "There are 33 million different versions of Netflix."

Case of AirBnB

Netflix is a great example of a company that is changing from a traditional business model to an AI factory. It shows how companies build their products. It showed how problem-solving loops work, the different shapes they can take, and how they can be used to make answers that focus on people. What makes this new way of designing different from other methods? In this way, the hospitality business is useful because it has a lot of competitors with both old-fashioned and AI-based ways of doing things.

Hospitality companies are naturally very hard to make people-centered because their customers come from a wide range of cultures, ages, backgrounds, and travel reasons. As an example of how complicated cultures can be, think about how Booking.com's chatbot can speak between 43 different languages. Due to this level of complexity, the industry's old way of doing things relied on big investments in real estate (hotels and their rooms and spaces) and processes that required a lot of work from people who had to be hired, trained, and organized. Because of this, companies with a lot of assets need to plan their rooms in a more or less standard way, and they stay that way for a long time. The user experience and the back-end of the service are also planned and formalized so that they can be provided to users with high quality standards. Providing experiences that are tailored to each person is very hard with this operational model. To deal with these problems, the industry has seen some of the most common and well-known efforts to combine design thinking techniques in the last few decades. In the business world, IDEO's work for Intercontinental Hotels Group is an example of a design thinking endeavor. One project, for instance, was aimed at short-stay tourists and wanted to make things easy for them in a way that could be done reliably and consistently. Business visitors were the focus of another project that led to the creation of good places to work and meet. Another one was all about making the Holiday Inn Express brand look and feel better by changing everything from how you check in to how the rooms look and feel. Using standard operating models, all of these projects followed a linear design process: ethnography to understand the needs of stakeholders, ideation to create good experiences for the target group, and rough prototyping for the solutions that were found. Innovation labs, which are large rooms where design teams can make 1:1 scale prototypes of rooms and try out new ideas before putting them into action on a larger scale, have become popular in this field as a way to bring about innovation. Marriott and Hilton chose real hotels to run B-tests, where customers could directly get in touch with new ideas and give a more accurate assessment of the suggested innovation. Sometimes, room design innovation was taken to the extreme, and it was done right there on the hotel property. After that, the projects were set in stone in terms of the rooms, processes, and IT programs that the asset-heavy operating system could deliver in a consistent and correct way on a large scale.

At the end of the 2000s, the hotel industry started to change in a big way. As new companies with simpler ways of doing business joined the market, they ran into old businesses that relied on a lot of assets. Both Marriott and Airbnb let guests who need it stay in their own rooms. By letting hosts run the business, Airbnb got around the problems that come with standard operating systems, like having to build more rooms than needed to handle growth. Two things determine whether AirBnB can provide a cutting-edge service that is tailored to each user's specific wants, and this at a large scale. First, the creative ways that designs can be made. For example, Airbnb, which started in 2007, had more than 3 million hosts in more than 190 countries and 80,000 places in 2017. That's three times the number of rooms at Marriott International, which has been around since 1927. Even better, each of these 3 million rooms was different. Three million different styles. It would not have been possible for design firms in the traditional asset-heavy business to offer such a wide range of choices and creative solutions in physical design. Second, this huge amount of creativity had to be linked to what each person needed. This is where AI Factories come in handy. When you use AirBnB, the company gathers a huge amount of information about you. The data science team added a lot of logging to the booking flow in 2016. This lets AirBnB learn about what guests see, how they interact with different types of interfaces, how long they stay on a listing page, how long it takes them to make a booking request, and the exact time they decide to go back to search. A new event log is sent to a central store every time a customer uses Airbnb's search engine. As these logs add up, they give a detailed picture of the customer, including her likes and dislikes and how she acts. Airbnb immediately ends the problem-solving loop when a customer returns to the service looking for a new travel experience. Data is taken from the repository and processed by an AI-engine to create a new solution that is tailored not only to the customer but also to the interaction. That's kind of how the system works, like how we talked about with Netflix. What's even more interesting is that Airbnb is a "two-sided market," which means it deals with two types of users in real time. Because of this, its AI machine has different problem-solving loops that work at the same time for each type of user. One way that Airbnb designs the price of each listing instantly and dynamically is by having hosts check a box allowing Airbnb's AI engine to use data streams to automatically refine the price of their accommodation within a price range. This is an example of a problem-solving loop that works best for the host. To figure out how customers are responding to price changes, the AI-engine looks at a huge amount of data from the ecosystem. This includes the change in the check-in lead time as the check-in date gets closer, the popularity of the post, and the history of bookings. The result is that the price is set each time a guest asks for that particular property.

AirBnB is able to provide user-centered experiences that are less affected by the problems that come up when trying to balance the needs of different stakeholders. This is possible because both sides of the platform are user-centered and use the same data lake for independent problem-solving loops. AirBnB quickly became a central node in its network thanks to this design approach. This meant that Airbnb's reputation went up, its user base got bigger because of more hosts, and it got more hosts because of the opposite effect. This is the best example of people-centeredness: it focused on each person, even those who fit into different user groups, in a way that made the answers better over time. It couldn't have been done with the way things are usually designed.

Discussion

As AI spreads through society, design professionals and experts are curious about how this will change how we think about design. How will it change the way we do design? If that's the case, will it even question its core beliefs? First, let's answer the first question.

Artificial Intelligence and Design Practice

As of now, digital technologies have mostly spread into how businesses work, cutting down on the time and money needed to make and transport goods and services. But the process of designing those goods and services was mostly done by people. Going back to Figure 1, the "designing" took a lot of time and money, even though the "making" was quick and easy. It had to be an action that happened only sometimes and for a small group of users through projects.

This situation changes a lot because of AI, which is important to people who study innovation because it brings digital technology upstream, into the area of design. These automation features can help designers do simple tasks more quickly, like they used to be able to do. To give you an example, Airbnb is working on an AI system that will help automate a common design task: turning mockups drawn by designers into part specs for software engineers. The method is based on all design parts being standardized and put into groups. AI can spot parts of Airbnb's designs that were probably drawn by hand on a piece of paper and turn them into specifications and source code for prototypes automatically.

As shown above, AI could only be used to automate design jobs that are already being done. This would not change the core of design practice. But the examples of Netflix and AirBnB that we talked about in the last session show that AI has a much bigger effect on design than just automating what designers already do; it completely changes the way they do their jobs. That is, AI marks the beginning of a big change in how we think about design.

The problem-solving skills built into AI are what make it possible to change the way design is done. They let algorithms make detailed design decisions that designers normally make, like what interface to show a user, what content to make, and how to place a product compared to competitors. This is made possible by machine learning. This has huge effects on both the thing being designed and the way it is designed.

The first major change is in the thing that designers work on (the "what" of design). Designers used to make solutions (like products, services, and experiences) that could be given to a lot of people. Designers planned and created everything a customer saw and did, right down to the smallest details, like a picture that would be shown on a screen. Instead, AI creates and delivers the exact solution that each person sees on their phone screen, as well as the solution that they experience, "in the moment." This is done by an AI-powered problem-solving loop. To put it another way, designers don't come up with solutions for AI problems; they come up with loops for fixing those problems.

This change in object has effects that are upsetting. This is especially true since most AI programs don't think like designers do. This means they don't just copy what designers think; they work in a different way. Most of the applications we talked about in the Netflix and AirBnB cases are examples of "weak" AI, which means they are based on very simple tasks like recognizing a shape in an image or figuring out if two images have different shapes. This is different from what we usually think of as "strong AI," which mimics human behavior and reasoning. In simple terms, weak AI is "dumb" by nature. However, weak AI can make complex predictions that are even better than human abilities by doing these jobs millions of times and feeding them huge amounts of data. At least in terms of how much it costs and how quickly it can be solved.

The effects on design students and teachers are very strong. How do you make loops that solve problems? How do you come up with design rules that are based on very easy tasks but, when repeated over and over, can give users very complex solutions on their own? This is not how designers are taught. Their minds are trained to handle complicated jobs in a structured way. To use AI's full potential, they need to be able to picture what a dumb system can do when it works on a large scale.

When you change the goal of your design (from making answers to making problem-solving loops), so does the process (the "how" of design). This is clear when we look at Figure 1 next to Figure 2, which was shown earlier: When it comes to AI Factories, the planning process is broken up into two parts. First, a design phase that involves a lot of people coming up with ideas for the solution space and how to solve problems; next, an AI-powered phase where an algorithm comes up with a solution that works for each person. Since the second part of the process doesn't cost much and doesn't take long, the development of the solution can begin for each customer at the exact moment she requests it. This, in turn, lets us use the newest data and learning to make a better, more original answer every time. Now there is no longer a blueprint for a product or service that stands between creation and use. Design, delivery, and use all happen at the same time or almost at the same time.

There is a clear example of this new trend in software-based digital experiences like Netflix and AirBnB, but it is also spreading to businesses that make physical products. Let's look at the case of Tesla. It works like Netflix or

Airbnb in that it collects a lot of data from devices inside and outside the car to create personalized experiences for each user. To make problem-solving loops work, though, Tesla has to deal with a real problem: the car. Hardware creation can't happen in real time, from afar, or automatically yet. So, in order to use AI to its full potential, Tesla had to rethink how the car was built, going in two different ways. First, it got rid of all the real parts that could be used to interact with it. Instead, most of the controls were put into digital user interfaces, like the big touchscreen in the middle. Second, it put too many devices in cars to collect data. As well as data from internal monitors, data come from outside sources, like ultrasound equipment, GPS input, cameras, radar transmitters, and LIDAR. As cars move, sensors collect a lot of data to improve Telsa's datasets and teach its learning algorithms new things. It's interesting that some of these sensors are "silent," which means they aren't being used to directly help customers yet. Instead, they are being "placed in perspective." After the product comes out, they are turned on remotely to make room for new loops and give customers new services. Since 2017, the Model 3 has had a camera in the rearview mirror that faces the inside of the car. At first, this camera was not working. Thanks to new software updates, the camera was only able to spot people inside the car in June 2019. It then changes things like the seats, mirrors, music, and driving mode based on the user's profile.

Artificial Intelligence and Design Principles

In the setting of AI Factories, our examples show that design practice changes a lot, both in terms of what is designed and how it is designed. Does AI also go against the basic ideas that design is based on? To put it another way, is this new way of designing still focused on people, using deduction, and repeating? Or does it come from a different set of beliefs?

Based on what we've seen, AI doesn't seem to question the basic ideas behind design thought. Instead, it makes them stronger.

To back up this claim, we look at how AI gets rid of the problems that come with standard design that relies on people. More specifically, we begin with the results of an in-depth study of AI-powered tactics that was carried out by one of us. The research shows that AI changes the way a company works by getting rid of three problems: learning, scale, and scope. Let's look at how AI removes these barriers, allowing design to focus on people, build abductions, and come up with new ideas through iterations.

Scale and people centeredness. Traditional ways of designing had big problems with scale. It took a lot of time and money because it was one of the most intense human-based tasks. This was especially true during development, when many important decisions had to be made. Because of this, it wasn't practical to create an answer each time a user asked for one. Large engineer-to-order systems were the only ones whose price fully covered the cost of design. Other than those, solutions were made in the form of goods and services that were aimed at different users or groups of customers. During production and delivery, some customization was possible, but the design phase was only done on a few projects. During this phase, users were talked to in terms of typical archetypes, which is why "personas" are used in traditional design thought processes. Because of this, the limits of the scale made people-centeredness much harder to achieve.

With AI, there are no longer any big scale limits on design because machines are developing specific answers. First, these machines are built with design rules that put the person first. A lot of information about each person is used in supervised learning, as we saw with Netflix. Second, this focus on people can be stretched to fit any number of users or level of data complexity. Based on the user's own information, the detailed answer that she experiences (for example, what she sees on the Netflix app screen) was made just for her. It's interesting that the link between scale and focus on people has now been turned around. The more users there were and the more complicated the ideas, the harder it was to focus on each person in human-intensive design. When talking about AI factories, the machines get better at guessing how people will act the more users there are and the more complicated and rich the data stream is. AirBnB gives us an even more advanced version. In this situation, the group has to deal with both hosts and guests at the same time. The learning loops aren't hurt by this increase in complexity, and they even gain from the fact that data from both sides of the market is being used together. About scope and abductions. Human-centered design methods also had big limits on what they could do. The products were made for a certain business and consumer group. And the project idea probably wouldn't be used in a different setting once it was finished. A car was made to be a way to get around. It wasn't likely that they would move on to entertainment services. And if that was the case, a new offering had to be made. Even in the same business, limitations in scope were big problems. Take a look at the example of design thought at Intercontinental Hotels Group that was given earlier. The solution IDEO made for short-stay travelers (which was focused on convenience) and the solution they made for business travelers had to be designed by different teams and under different names within the same company. Abductions aren't possible very often because human-intense design has small fields of application. The design brief told us what the design area could include. Once the task was clear and set in stone, that was the only place where creativity could happen.

AI can get rid of limits on what can be done. A design brief in AI Factories is flexible and can be changed even after a product has been released. We've seen how Netflix uses unsupervised learning to find new trends in how its customers like to watch TV shows that weren't planned at the start of the process. People use these statements to back up abductions when they're making up new movie series. With this kind of flexible scope in the design, it may be possible to explore completely new design areas. As an example, AirBnB has grown into "travel experiences" by letting guests do things like rent bands or go horseback riding on the beach. The same AI factory that powers AirBnB's standard hospitality service is used to get into this new business. Tesla also uses the learning loops built into its cars to add fun to its main service (transportation) that people can enjoy while they're traveling. AI factories don't have any limits on what they can do, which made it possible for a car company to come up with a revolutionary idea.

Learning and iterations. Finally, traditional design methods had problems that made it harder to learn. In fact, the design-build-test cycles that help people learn were limited to a single job. Iterations stopped happening for the most part once the project was over and the result was made available. Seeing how real people use a product can teach us new things that can only help us make better versions in the future. Innovation happened in chunks and spurts. And as things changed, quickly, new answers became "old."

AI takes away a lot of the barriers to learning. Keep in mind that AI companies are naturally iterative. Their delivery is done in loops. In the case of Netflix, the company starts a problem-solving loop every time a customer uses the service. This loop doesn't just use the newest data and methods. It also gives you a chance to learn something new. When the algorithm is used, it can tell the learning strategy to make things better, like changing its parameters to show a better movie cover to a certain user, or to look for new opportunities, like suggesting a new movie category to that user. This balancing act of exploring and exploiting is made easier by reinforcement learning and double-armed bandit algorithms. It happens all the time, throughout the life cycle of a product. There are big effects on creativity because of this.

First, you can always learn more. A certain user's answer at a certain time is different from the solution she had when the product first came out. It's the most advanced plan we've seen so far. The answer is always "new" in a way. This is possible in part because software-run experiences are naturally flexible and can sometimes include new releases made by software workers. Design, build, and test are all steps in the learning loop that are done automatically in AI Factories. What this means is that every time a customer uses a service, a new version of the product is "released." The second way to learn is through real-life use. It used to be that people learned by testing samples in simple or safe situations. Now, people learn by actually using the product in its current circumstance. Third, learning is focused on the person. In the past, the experience given to a certain person was based on what was learned from other people, such as from customers who used older versions of a product or from users who tried a prototype. Now, insights use information from both the person and other buyers or clients. For the fourth time, each release is a chance to not only keep making the design better, but also to try new things and make room for bigger innovations. In order to do this, learning loops are made in a way that is different from how other goods are made. The second one had only the traits that were thought to be useful at the time it was made. In AI Factories, on the other hand, the planned loops are crowded with parts that aren't fully used when the game comes out. In other words, AI factories are purposely built with redundant features. For example, in the case of Tesla, sensors that will allow self-driving cars are used to teach algorithms about the complexity and variety of real-life street situations, even though most of their features are still not available or the internal pointing camera has not actively delivered any feature for two years.

In short, AI Factories adds to and strengthens the design thought principles: It's not just about people; it's also about one person; it encourages creativity across segments, stakeholders, and industries, allowing abductions beyond what a product was originally designed for; and finally, it's always iterative, bringing learning and innovation into the whole product life cycle, not just during development.

Design for Artificial Intelligence

If AI makes design more advanced, then design can make AI more successful and focused on people. Take the hotel business as an example. Booking.com and AirBnB both use AI a lot, for example to make listings more personal and to help hosts decide on prices. Booking.com, on the other hand, comes up with new ideas less through design and more through a lot of A/B testing. So, at Booking.com, features are pushed "from the lab outwards" instead of "from the user-inwards." The other side is AirBnB. Two of its owners, Brian Chesky and Joe Gebbia, went to the Rhode Island School of Design and learned design thinking there. The Snow White project was started by the company in 2011 to bring human-centered design to all levels of the business and change the way they compete. Rebecca Sinclair, who was Head of User Experience Research and Design at the time and had worked as a designer at IDEO, was in charge of the project. Sinclair says, "Like many tech startups at the time, we called the website and the app 'the product.'" However, "by using design thinking [...] we looked at a journey [...] imagining our customers booking, and we saw that the most important parts were when they weren't online." They didn't buy a website or an app; they bought this real-life event, like a trip to Paris or a stay in a treehouse. Then we started to say, "The product is the trip," and our view began to change. One way to see how this design approach has led to innovation is to look at the user interfaces of AirBnB and Booking.com. Another way is to look at how AirBnB has used AI to create new business categories like Airbnb Experiences.

Microsoft gives us another look at the important part that design plays in putting artificial intelligence to use. Satya Nadella, the CEO of Microsoft, said that AI is the new "runtime" of the company. Its business plan is now based on AI. Because of this, the company had to completely reorganize its IT and data assets, which were spread out among its different business units. It's interesting that the change wasn't led by an IT boss or an expert in IT. Instead, the project was led by Kurt Del Bene, an executive with product experience who used to be the head of Microsoft's Office business unit, and a group of leaders and engineers from product roles. Nadella did want the way the company worked and the AI Factory to be set up so that they were more like building goods than IT systems.

Artificial Intelligence and Design Theories

In 1988, Mihaly Csikszentmihalyi and Herbert Simon began arguing about what creativity really is in light of progress in computer intelligence and the questions it raised about how we think about thinking. When Simon and his colleagues at Carnegie Mellon University looked into the possibilities of a computer program called "BACON," they were supporting a logical view of how the mind works (Simon, 1985), which said that creativity could be seen as a way of solving problems, which means that computers are partly involved in this process. Another chapter by Csikszentmihalyi (1988a) disagreed with this view: "Simon wants to prove that creativity is only problem-solving." Csikszentmihalyi suggested that "problem-finding is the hallmark of creativity." Csikszentmihalyi's challenge made Simon's point even stronger in 1988: "I would claim that, just as finding laws that explain data is a problem-solving process, so finding good problems and relevant data for solving them are normal problem-solving processes." The main point of Csikszentmihalyi's answer is in the first sentence of this section: finding problems and fixing them are not the same thing. He thought about how design ideas would change over the next few years. On the one hand, there were scholars who saw design mostly as a way to solve creative problems. However, researchers who saw design as a way of organizing problems or, to be more specific, as making sense of things.

In the last few decades, most of the attention in the creation of theories has been on the first stream, which is creative problem solving. It also included how to frame a problem (like in the double diamond model of Design Thinking), but it was still based on Simon's ideas about how to solve problems (where problem framing was still seen as a logical step in nested problem solution). This direction of theory development was deemed appropriate because solving problems was hard and needed a lot of work from people. The present spread of AI is making this situation very different. More and more, AI factories are using automatic learning loops to include problem-solving. This means that framing and making sense are now at the heart of human design.

There are important theoretical effects. Let's start with the ideas of how to solve problems. Most of these theories, especially those that deal with Design Thinking, were created with the idea that people can solve problems related to creation. What happen when computers figure them out? For example, we've already talked about how AI loops work by repeating simple, "weak" rules, and how creators should instead look at complex problems as a whole. Another example has to do with the moral effects of loops: they grow very quickly and exponentially, leading to large-scale unwanted effects like making biases stronger. How to give artists the right frames to see ahead of time how their design will have an exponential effect?

A second, even more important conclusion is that we need to change the theoretical lenses we use to look at design as a human activity. Design is not just about solving problems (which machines are doing more and more of these days), but also and especially about making sense of things. AI Factories need designers to figure out what problems are most important to solve, then create the learning loops, and finally make sure that the loops keep changing in a way that makes sense. Just to give you a simple example that Csikszentmihalyi used in his talk with Simon: If an algorithm was made to fix a problem, it can't refuse to do so; it can't "pull the plug" (unless this feature is already built into its code). A person can. It is possible to avoid designing something if it doesn't make sense on a moral, social, or personal level.

Because researchers have mostly been interested in fixing problems, we still don't fully understand how design can be used to make sense. So, there is a huge (and interesting) space ahead that needs to be studied.

We think that the most important theoretical advances in design thinking will come from studying problem framing in more depth and using ideas of making sense of things. We also think that design will become more like leadership, which is an essential part of making sense.

Conclusions

AI is different from all other digital technologies. It does more than just schedule tasks. It makes learning automatic, which is what creativity is all about. Because of this, it provides never-before-seen chances to greatly lower the cost and time of creating a new answer. In this chapter, we looked at the strategies of Netflix, Airbnb, Tesla, and Microsoft, four companies that were ahead of their time in AI, to get a sense of what this means for design.

Based on the cases, it looks like AI doesn't go against the ideas and theories behind Design Thinking. Instead, it removes old limits on scale, scope, and learning, which makes design even more fundamental: it creates the most person-centered experiences that can be tailored to each person and continuously improved based on their data; AI may boost creativity by broadening the design space beyond product categories and industries; and finally, it makes iterations and experiments central to how businesses work.

However, AI Factories' creation process is very different from what we were used to. We've created a framework to talk about this change and show what design means in the new AI Factories setting. Since artificial intelligence came along, computers are now doing a lot of the problem-solving and what we used to call "development." Their learning loops help them keep coming up with new ideas and looking for better ways to do things. When these algorithms are run thousands or even millions of times, they can solve very complicated problems. This is because they think in terms of small, simple processes that can be repeated over and over again.

Because of this, it is very important for managers to understand how design works differently now that AI is around, so they don't apply the right design concepts (which don't change) to the wrong process (which does).

For scholars, the effects on design ideas are also very important. Two new kinds of structures are needed. First, we need to give designers new models to help them with their new job, which is not to design answers but to design the problem-solving loops that will lead to solutions. Second, and this is more important for managing design and innovation, we need to learn more about the strategic side of design, which is setting a meaningful path. In AI Factories, the human side of planning is turning into more and more of a matter of making sense (figuring out which problems make sense to solve). At this point, design is more connected to management, and more specifically to leading innovation. In a way, the gap between design and management has been getting smaller for about twenty years now. In the past, though, management theory was the one that went closer to design in search of new ways to help people solve problems.

Our hope now is that design will become more connected to management. And the gap will get smaller in a new way: the way we make sense of things. There is a lot of room for mixing ideas between the two fields, especially between design (with its theories of framing and critique) and leadership (with its theories of making sense and dialogic). This space is important, largely untapped, and it looks like it will be one of the most interesting journeys for innovation scholars in the years to come.

References

Boland, R.J. and F. Collopy. 2004. Managing as Designing. Palo Alto: Stanford Business Books. Brown, T. 2008. Design thinking. Harvard business review 86(6): 1-10.

Brown, T. 2009. Change by design: How design thinking transforms organisations and inspires innovation. New York: Harper Business Press.

Buchanan, R. 1992. Wicked Problems in Design Thinking. Design Issues 8(2): 5-21. Carr, D. 2013. Giving viewers what they want. Available at: https://www.nytimes.com/2013/02/25/business/media/for-house-of-cards-using-big-data-to- guarantee-its-popularity.html

Chandrashekar, A., F. Amat, J. Basilico and T. Jebara. 2017. Artwork Personalization at Netflix. Available at: https://netflixtechblog.com/artwork-personalization-c589f074ad76

Chang, R. 2017. Using Machine Learning to Predict Value of Homes On Airbnb. Available at: https://medium.com/airbnb-engineering/using-machine-learning-to-predict-value-of-homes- on-airbnb-9272d3d4739d

Csikszentmihalyi, M. (1988a). Motivation and creativity: Toward a synthesis of structural and energistic approaches to cognition. New Ideas in psychology 6(2): 159-176.

Csikszentmihalyi, M. (1988b). Solving a problem is not finding a new one: A reply to Simon. New Ideas in Psychology 6(2): 183-186.

Dai, P. 2017. Helping Guests Make Informed Decisions with Market Insights. Available at: https://medium.com/airbnb-engineering/helping-guests-make-informed-decisions-with- market-insights-8b09dc904353

Domingos, P. 2012. A few useful things to know about machine learning. Communications of the ACM 55(10): 78-87.

Dorst, K. 2015. Frame Innovation. Creating New Thinking by Design. Cambridge: MIT Press.

Elsbach, K. and I. Stigliani. 2018. Design Thinking and Organizational Culture: A Review and Framework for Future Research. Journal of Management 44(6): 2274—306.

Galle, P. 2002. Philosophy of design: an editorial introduction. Design Studies 23(3): 211—218.

Gibson, J. J. 1977, 'The theory of affordances,' in R., Shaw and J. Bransford (eds), Perceiving, Acting, and Knowing. Toward an Ecological Psychology. Lawrence Erlbaum: Hillsdale, NJ: 67—82.

Iansiti, M. and K. Lakhani. 2020. Competing in the Age of Artificial Intelligence. Cambridge, MA: Harvard Business Press.

Jahnke, M. 2013. Meaning in the Making: Introducing a Hermeneutic Perspective on the Contribution of Design Practice to Innovation. Gothenburg: University of Gothenburg.

Kelley, D. and T. Kelley. 2013. Creative Confidence: Unleashing the Creative Potential within Us All. New York: Crown Publishing.

Krippendorff, K. 1989. On the Essential Contexts of Artifacts or on the Proposition that "design is Making Sense (of Things)". Design Issues 5(2): 9-38.

Krippendorff, K. 2006. The Semantic Turn: A New Foundation for Design. Boca Raton: CRC Press. Lambert, F. 2017. Tesla Model 3 is equipped with a driver-facing camera for Autopilot and Tesla Network. Available at: https: / /electrek.co/2017/08/01/tesla-model-3-driver-facing-camera- autopilot-tesla-network/

Lambert, F. 2018. Tesla will have a KITT-like artificial intelligence in its vehicles, says Elon Musk. Available at: https://electrek.co/2018/07/29/tesla-kitt-like-artificial-intelligence-elon-musk/

Lambert, F. 2019. Tesla reveals how it will use camera inside Model 3 to personalize in-car experience. Available at: https://electrek.co/2019/07/24/tesla-use-camera-inside-cars-personalize-in-car- experience/

Leister, R.K., M.J. Piore and K.M. Malek. 2002. Interpretive Management: What General Managers Can Learn from Design. Harvard Business Review 76(2): 86-96.

Liedtka, J. 2015. Perspective: Linking design thinking with innovation outcomes through cognitive bias reduction. Journal of Product Innovation Management 32(6): 925—938.

Love, T. 2000. Philosophy of design: a metatheoretical structure for design theory. Design Studies 21(3): 293-313.

Margolin, Victor 1989. Design Discourse: History, Theory and Criticism. Chicago: University of Chicago Press. Margolin, V. and R. Buchanan. 1996. The Idea of Design. Cambridge: The MIT Press.

Martin, R. 2009. The Design of Business: Why Design Thinking Is the Next Competitive Advantage. Boston: Harvard Business Press.

Mayfield, J., K. Puttaswamy, S. Jagadish and K. Long. 2016. Data Infrastructure at Airbnb. Available at: https://medium.com/airbnb-engineering/data-infrastructure-at-airbnb-8adfb34f169c

Micheli, P., S.J. Wilner, S.H. Bhatti, M. Mura and M.B. Beverland. 2019. Doing design thinking: Conceptual review, synthesis, and research agenda. Journal of Product Innovation Management 36(2): 124-148.

Norman, D.A. and R. Verganti. 2014. Incremental and Radical Innovation: Design Research vs. Technology and Meaning Change. Design Issues 30(1): 78-96.

Orlikowski, W.J. 2010. Practice in research: phenomenon, perspective and philosophy. In Cambridge Handbook of Strategy as Practice, ed. D. Golsorkhi, L. Rouleau, D. Seidl and E. Vaara, 23-33. Cambridge: Cambridge University Press.

Saarinen, K. 2017. Building a Visual Language: Behind the scenes of our new design system. Available at: https://airbnb.design/building-a-visual-language/

Schleifer, A. 2017. The Way We Build: How rethinking the Airbnb app changed the way we approach design. Available at: https://airbnb.design/the-way-we-build/

Seidel, V. P., and S. K. Fixson. 2013. Adopting design thinking in novice multidisciplinary teams: The application and limits of design methods and reflexive practices. Journal of Product Innovation Management 30(1): 19—33.

Simon, H.A. 1982. The Sciences of the Artificial. Cambridge: The MIT Press.

Simon, H.A. 1988. Creativity and motivation: A response to Csikszentmihalyi. New Ideas in psychology 6(2): 177-181.

Spangler, T. 2018. Netflix Eyeing Total of About 700 Original Series in 2018. Available at: https://variety.com/2018/digital/news/netflix-700-original-series-2018-1202711940

Srinivasan, S. 2018. Learning Market Dynamics for Optimal Pricing: Combining elements of machine learning with structural modeling. Available at: https://medium.com/airbnb-engineering/learning-market-dynamics-for-optimal-pricing-97cffbcc53e3

Stigliani, I. and D. Ravasi. 2012. Organizing thoughts and connecting brains: Material practices and the transition from individual to group-level prospective sensemaking. Academy of Management Journal 55(5): 1232-1259.

Verganti, R. 2008. Design, meanings, and radical innovation: A meta-model and a research agenda. Journal of Product Innovation Management 25(5): 436-456.

Verganti, R. 2009. Design-driven innovation — Changing the rules of competition by radically innovating what things mean. Boston: Harvard Business Press.

Verganti, R. 2011a. Designing Breakthrough Products. Harvard Business Review 89(10): 114-120.

Verganti, R. 2011b. Radical Design and Technology Epiphanies: a new focus for research on design management. Journal ofProduct Innovation Management 28(3): 384-388.

Verganti, R. and A. Oberg. 2013. Interpreting and Envisioning: A Hermeneutic Framework to Look at Radical Innovation of Meanings. Industrial Marketing Management 42(1): 86-95.

Wilson, M. 2015. Inside The Hip Redesign Of Holiday Inn Express: Ideo helps the budget hotel chain rethink everything from beds to mood lighting. Available at: https://www.fastcompany.com/3043478/inside-the-hip-redesign-of-holiday-inn-express

Chapter 2
User Experience Design in the AI Age

Introduction

Norman said that design is a conversation between the designer and the user. He also said that good design takes a deep understanding of human psychology and needs. When making a digital product or service, designers must think about how the user will feel while using it. People who use digital solutions also have high standards for how well an app or service works and how nice it looks. They also expect designers to be able to understand those needs and translate them into useful features and nice looks. It has been shown that an iterative product development life cycle, high-quality creativity, user research, and usability tasks can work together to make creative and easy-to-use solutions. In spite of that, it still takes a lot of work, understanding, and time. The job is made even harder by the fact that designers have to figure out right away what needs to be made (issue setting) and build the solution (problem-solving).

In the past few years, big steps forward in artificial intelligence (AI) and machine learning (ML) have had a big effect on user experience (UX) practices, making it easier to offer solutions with better UX. It's becoming clearer that using AI to improve UX design processes is a clear trend that can lead to new job chances for people who work in the field. Notably, some experts say that "AI/ML is the new UX" and want a big shift in the way things are done. In this case, the trend shows how AI and ML are changing the user experience landscape, which opens up many possibilities for UX designers.

AI has been getting a lot of attention lately, according to both researchers and digital designers. This is because it opens up a lot of new design possibilities and makes UX designers' jobs easier by saving them time and effort. On the other hand, AI should have been looked at in terms of what it can and can't do, as well as social concerns. Digital designers also need to keep their skills and knowledge up to date to keep up with AI's progress and how it affects UX/UI design.

The way UX designers do their work has already changed a lot since AI technology has grown. It is very important to know how these technologies can be made to help people find what they want and work well with the planning process. As AI has grown, it has opened up interesting new ways to improve the UX design process. These ways can be used for simple tasks like filtering spam and for more complicated tasks like self-driving cars. AI claims to both make the user experience better and create new ways of interacting that were not possible before.

Even so, putting AI into the UX design process has been seen as a possible risk, leading to worries about loss of control, autonomy, and harmony, as well as problems with performance. As a result of worries about losing their jobs, designers are also more stressed out and unhappy. It is thought that to get the most out of AI in UX design, you need to have a deep knowledge of both technical and human factors.

The point of this chapter is to look at existing academic literature to find out how AI has changed UX design over the past few years and what challenges and opportunities it brings up so that future study can be guided.

The rest of this chapter is organized into six pieces. The next part, "Background," will give you an overview of the most important related work on AI definition and the design process. This chapter also looks at how well the written plan works at improving the UX using AI. Section III: Research Questions is the next part, which lists the study's research questions and goals. After that, the Methodology section will explain how the research was done, and the Findings and Discussion section will talk about the research questions in light of the literature study.

Background

UX design process

Voil says that the most important parts of UX should be thought about when making or testing a product. Design is the part of creativity that deals with choices and how people come up with ideas and solve problems. And describe design practice as "the experience of design in a certain setting, including how decisions are made about designs (through what steps, methods, tools, or collaborative work) and the goal of design (what designs are made and what new solutions it creates, such as a good, service, or process)". Finally, describe design principle as "the perspective and philosophy that guide the act of designing and make up an ontology of what design is."

In the past few years, a lot of attention has been paid to the process of creating the UX. Schmidt and Etches say that UX design is "the process of supporting user behavior through usability, usefulness, and desirability while interacting with a product." Sticking to a clear and well-known process that includes important steps like piloting, testing, and improving is an important part of UX design. User-centered design is also a process structure that puts customers at the center of product design and development. This makes it one of the most popular ways to make digital solutions more enjoyable for users.

Intentions are the user's goals and tasks that make them want to interact with the system. Predispositions are the user's personal traits that affect how they see and react to the system. Environment is the physical and technical setting in which the user interacts with the system. Social setting and structure are the social and organizational setting in which the user works or operates. And finally, reflexivity is the feedback loop between the user's experience and their predispositions. These other UX features can be seen in Figure 1.

Figure 1. Model of UX design

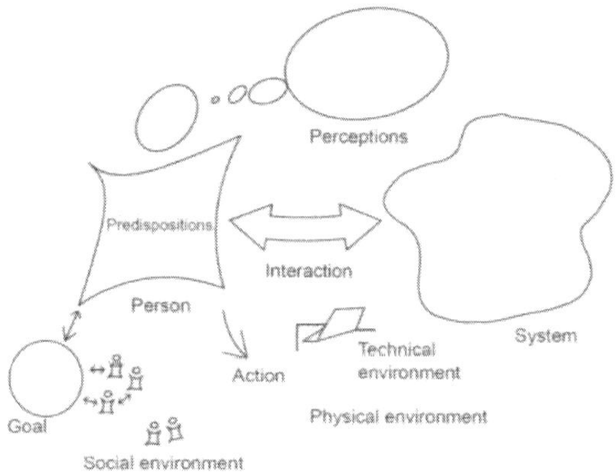

UX design process

Although there are many other meanings of AI, Norman's was the most complete and all-encompassing. He said that AI is mainly about the intelligence shown by artificial beings. This kind of intelligence includes things like being able to see, think, learn, communicate, and work in complicated situations. One of AI's long-term goals is to make tools that can do these jobs just as well as people, if not better.

More and more AI is being used in design, which has led to a wide range of changing conceptual models. Not only do these conceptual models give broad explanations of AI's part in design, they also include measures of how well it does things like coming up with new ideas. This group of ideas includes the idea of "artificial design intelligence" (ADI). Using machine learning methods, these AI systems have gained a deep understanding of design, which lets them predict design trends and come up with design solutions before anyone else does.

Also, using AI in UX design means giving computers human-like abilities to do tasks that need human intelligence. This is because AI has strengths like allowing customization on a large scale, accurate analysis of how digital solutions are used, and helping designers come up with new ideas. To begin, AI has many advantages. Solutions not only make products easier to use and more interactive, which boosts productivity, but they also help predict user happiness, which is a key factor in users' choices about whether to use a product or service again or tell others about it. Second, AI can be used to make traditional machine learning models work better by making the model with smaller sample sizes. This means that AI methods can be used to help UX designers deal with the problems they face when they use AI in their work.

a. **AI as a new design material**: As AI technology develops, experts in UX design are constantly integrating AI capabilities into the creation of new applications, devices, and systems. AI is gradually becoming easier to access so that non-experts, like UX professionals, may make use of it. A significant change in this dynamic environment is the idea that intelligence is a new kind of material for design.

Right now, improving end users' skills is becoming the main job of UX designers. Designers are actively looking into how AI can be used as a design feature and how it might improve the UX design as a whole. They are working together with AI teams from different departments across the company and promoting new ideas at both the system and service levels. However, it can be hard for designers to show that AI functions are worth the money they cost. People who work in user experience (UX) are also having trouble explaining AI ideas clearly. For now, they are just playing around with AI models to see what risks and benefits might come with using AI in their plans. For UX-driven ideation, UX designers often don't have the right tools because they work with models that have already been taught. They are constantly looking for more information about AI models and openness so that they can make smart choices about how to use AI.

The idea behind AI as a design material says that designers should think of AI as a capability similar to an application service in the fields of Human-Computer Interaction (HCI) and User Experience (UX). The purpose of this functionality is to offer unique user experiences by being designed to do specific tasks, like adding a "search" feature. What this means is especially important when it comes to apps with conversational user experiences. Researchers are still looking into the best ways to use AI as a design factor in user experience (UX) design. Researchers say that AI is a key part of how people deal with a system, since data gives us useful information about people and businesses and algorithms set rules for how things should work.

A new study on AI and design innovation says that when designers are thinking of new ideas, they should focus on well-known AI features that are likely to make the user experience better instead of thinking about complicated AI uses. Augmented user interfaces (AUIs) make this possible by letting designers build user scenarios and transactional flows while also being able to easily spot common and repeating user behaviors. This is especially helpful for business apps because it makes it easy to figure out how much time adaptation saves and how much time a worker spends on it. Our research builds on these findings by looking into how experienced designers use AI to come up with design ideas in more depth.

b. **AI for enhancing UX**: AI is being used to improve User Experience by offering deep understanding, customised assistance, and natural user communication. It is used in many different approaches, such as recommender systems, intelligent tutoring systems, and virtual assistants. The development of transparent, comprehensible, and equitable AI systems that prioritise user control, protect user data privacy, and promote diversity and inclusivity is at the core of AI for UX breakthroughs. AI technology can enhance UX design, design evaluation, user research, and user interaction with computing systems. AI algorithms can be used in user research projects to extract variables and find patterns for competitive advantages and brand positioning.

Ekstrand et al. also want to improve the user experience by looking at how people understand how well a program works. To do this, things like happiness, correctness, diversity, originality, and customization had to be evaluated. The results show how important it is to think about these things when creating a structural equation model and studying how well an algorithm works.

Recently, Willemsen et al. looked into user choice overload in recommender systems in a different study. The researchers found that the number of options presented changed the amount of work needed to make a choice. Users were happier with options when they had a lot of different ones to choose from, but that wasn't always the case.

c. **Challenges and future work of AI in UX**: Despite concerted efforts to integrate AI into UX design, designers encounter significant challenges in assimilating AI into established design paradigms. One major obstacle arises in the realm of UX/UI prototyping, where adopting an AI- centric approach complicates the customary process. Convincing leadership to embrace innovative designs becomes challenging, given the substantial volume of data required for AI-based prototyping. This poses difficulties for designers in demonstrating the value of their designs through functional prototypes, deviating from conventional practices. Recent research, Abbas et al underscores the lack of integration between UX and AI. UX designers struggle to collaborate with data scientists, facing a shortage of tools and skills for sketching or prototyping with AI.

Furthermore, many AI-based study projects have only had a small effect on academia, with few real-world effects on how businesses work. We don't fully understand how AI algorithms and UX work together yet, and it's hard to imagine what improvements AI might be able to make to UX. To close this gap, we need research that focuses on what practitioners really need, along with tools that can help them use new technologies and academic findings.

Abbas et al. say that AI is still not fully integrated into design patterns, schooling, and prototype tools, which means it is not being fully used to help designers. Existing tools are still in their early stages and can't answer all possible questions. They were also not made with UX designers in mind. AI-based prototyping tools are mostly made for software workers, which can be hard for people who don't know much about AI. A lot of study needs to be done to make prototyping tools that are specifically made for UX designers. These tools would help make prototypes quickly, find design problems early on, and lower the risks of product development. In the future, new AI-based design paradigms will need tools that take into account UX designers' knowledge base and how they think, making it easier for them to work together with AI/software engineers in real design settings. While AI can't take the place of UX designers' creative skills, it can be used to help with design and as a partner in co-creative UX design.

Research Questions

The purpose of this study is to look at the current state of literature reviews and come up with a clear research question. The goal is to get a much more accurate estimate of the remaining defects, learn important things, and define the path for future research. To fully achieve these benefits, the study will look at what is already known about AI for UX design by answering the six questions in Table 1.

Methdology

A literature review of eleven papers is done in this study to look at and rate the latest research on AI for UX design. Literature reviews are very important for finding all the relevant empirical evidence that meets certain inclusion criteria. This gives us a full picture of the study problem. Reviewing the literature on the effects of a phenomenon in different settings and methods can help you figure out if the phenomenon is stable or if there are other sources of variation. Using statistical methods to combine data increases the chance of finding real effects, but it can also show small biases.

Based on Kitchenham's instructions for how to do book reviews. Planning the review, doing the review, and writing up the review are the three steps that make up a literature review.

Planning the literature review

This step-by-step literature review process is set up to help you choose reliable and relevant literature. The terms are very important for helping with certain things. First, a list of terms is given. The keywords used in this study are shown in Figure 2. Second, the terms are ranked so that they can be searched on Scopus, ACM, WOB, IEEE Explore, Google Scholar, Digital Library, ResearchGate (RG), and EBSCO databases. Finally, all the literature has been gathered and will be studied to find important, useful, and valuable literature in the next step.

Figure 2. Research keywords

Conducting a literature review

At this point, a number of pieces of literature are being turned down because they don't meet certain standards. For instance, choosing literature that isn't relevant to AI supporting the UX process, giving priority to scholarly and peer-reviewed articles to make sure the information is reliable, valid, and of high quality, only looking at publications that came out after 2017 and excluding literature that wasn't written in English, and so on. Table 2 shows eleven pieces that give you general information that you can use to do more research and critical thinking.

Reporting a literature review

The goals of this stage are to look into the research questions listed in Table 1, give an overview of the results, and start a conversation about the gaps in the current literature to help guide future research.

Finding and Discussion

This chapter's literature review shows how AI-supported UX processes have been studied around the world in the past few years, focusing on studies done in Asia, Europe, and the United States. This research is based on eleven studies that were conducted between 2017 and 2023, but some studies use systematic literature review methods that include looking at over 100 more papers. As AI technology has grown, there has been a lot of interesting study on how it improves UX design. This may have led to a big change in the way people work. AI is known for its ability to improve innovation performance in terms of how well it focuses on the customer, how creative it is, and how fast it innovates overall.

To answer the research questions of the study, a full analysis of 11 identified studies has been done in this part. In line with the study questions, six main themes have come to light. The first goal of the research is to find the most common problems that come up during the UX design process (RQ1). The study also looks at the newest developments in artificial intelligence (AI) tools that have made big differences in user experience design (RQ2). Additionally, the research aims to find ways to improve user experiences in design by encouraging AI and people to work together (RQ3). Through the use of AI tools, the study also aims to find ways to improve the user experience process (RQ4). In order to fill in the gaps in the current research, this study looks into the relationship between AI and UX (RQ5) and the most common ways to test how AI and UX processes work together. Lastly, the study wants to give suggestions on how to improve the user experience process using AI tools (RQ6) and possible directions for more research to be done in the future.

a. What are the challenges encountered by UX designers in the integration of AI within the context of UX design?

Recently, the UX process has been very important for making sure that digital goods and services meet user expectations and needs. It does this by controlling how a person acts, thinks, and feels about a product. In the meantime, UX designers are having to deal with a number of problems. Also, some problems might happen more often than others.

a. **Challenges of design**: According to the current literature analysis, design is the most challenging sector of the UX process. Firstly, it is usually part of design-making decisions. For example, making decisions on the functional shape of an object or the intricacies of a product interface is frequently challenging for UX designers, they additionally have to choose which information to present on a screen, and Stige et al found UX design misalignment refers to a situation where the user UX design of a product or service does not align with the intended objectives, goals, or expectations. This can result in confusion, frustration, and reduced user engagement since UX designers make decision-making mistakes.

Second, it can be hard for designers to get needs and describe problem states. There are many reasons to collect requirements, such as finding out the different and sometimes conflicting needs, goals, and limitations of the parties, as well as why the framework doesn't have clear ways for people to communicate, and how changes will affect deadlines and resources. It could happen because the success criteria aren't clear, users don't have enough access, or people assume solutions before they understand the problems in the part where they spot problem states.

Abbas et al. also found that UX designers don't have enough drawing and prototyping tools and skills. In the same way, Gupta says that the prototyping tools used in the industry right now don't have enough features and don't deal with some of the most important problems, like being easy to use, having the right functions, being able to represent things accurately, and being enforceable. This can make it harder for them to stay competitive and keep up with the changing needs of the industry.

b. **Challenges of control process and result**: The lack of control and autonomy in the UX process is a common challenge in the field of user

UX design. This refers to situations in which designers are not given the flexibility to choose their own design solutions. This can occur for a number of reasons, including organisational hierarchies, a lack of resources, or conflicting stakeholder interests. Choudhury argues that even though the UX design process is extremely successful, it may not always produce the desired results. This is due to the iterative nature of the process, making it hard to predict every outcome.

b. How is AI currently used to support or enhance the UX design process?

According to Boy, the user participating in the design process, the careful analysis of the context, designing for UX, and evaluation are integral parts of the UX design process. Consider the literature. AI appears to be capable of assisting with all aspect of the UX, particularly the design process.

a. **AI supports analyse the user and the context**: Stige et al found AI enables greater customisation at scale. AI algorithms can analyse large amounts of user data to understand individual preferences and behaviours, allowing for personalised customisation of digital solutions at scale. Therefore, AI could categorises user behaviour and predicts user behaviour to provide a more precise analysis of the usage of digital solutions. Similarly, Verganti argues that AI allows the development of highly user-centered solutions by taking advantage of its ability to continuously learn and adapt based on user input and feedback.

According to Yang et al, discovered that artificial intelligence-aided design (AIAD) technology can measure and improve user experience by collecting and analysing user behaviour data efficiently, as traditional methods like user interviews and observations can be time-consuming and inefficient. These are to develop a deep neural network model that can simulate the user's experience in operating a mobile application by aggregating and mapping features of user behaviour in connection and hidden layers. On the other hand, Abbas et al argue that it would not be effective if the designers lack of understanding of how to effectively work with AI as a design tool.

b. **AI supports routine designing activity**: When identifying routine designing activities most activities were found regarding the design inspiration and automation of routine activities. Table 3. depicts the most common way AI supports routine designing activities that were found in the pieces of literature.

Making decisions is the most important part of designing: Stige et al. are interested in how AI can help people make decisions. AI can give designers data-driven insights and suggestions that can help them make better choices about how to use digital solutions. Yildirim et al., on the other hand, say that designers had data-driven insights, but their experience and understanding of the past limited their views when working with AI.

An extensive body of study has shown that AI can automate boring tasks, freeing up workers to do more difficult and creative tasks. Abbas et al. say that AI systems can do the same tasks over and over again very accurately and quickly. Using machine learning algorithms to look for patterns and make predictions is how Stige et al. showed that AI can automate everyday jobs.

Literature often talks about matching graphical features in sketches to their digital counterparts,. It's possible that this is because of new AI-based design tools like Paper2Wire, Meta Morph, and DesignScape that help graphical user interface (GUI) designers move from paper mockups to digital wireframes. It makes it easier to move from sketching to digital design, making sure that the end product is consistent and accurate. It also keeps the design's overall visual cohesion and aesthetic appeal, which makes the user experience more pleasing to the eye. But some AI models are only taught with a small set of pictures. So, artists should think about AI models that are appropriate and useful for their work.

In addition, the literature study points out another trend that can help UX designers find design ideas. Verganti stresses the use of unsupervised learning algorithms to find natural groups in data, which can show patterns and structures that are hidden and might not be obvious to humans. This way of doing things helps designers find groups that are related, which makes it easier to come up with new design ideas. In support of this trend, Holmquist and Choudhury use deep learning advances and look at user statistics.

Zhang et al. found that AI automatically looks at parts of designs to find ones that don't follow set design rules. Giving designers feedback and ideas in real time during the design process to make sure they follow the rules; and helping to find potential violations by comparing the design to a set of rules or best practices that have already been established. These might help UX designers save time and effort by automating the process of finding and fixing violations of design rules.

AI can also make design improvements and optimizations in real time, so you can get feedback and make changes right away. This makes the design process more efficient and effective. It lets artists quickly change and improve their designs based on what users say and how their needs change. If AI technologies are used in the design process, designers might have more time for study, exploration, and making big decisions.

AI helps with evaluation: The review is one of the most important parts. This needs to be done quickly and right. AI can be made to help UX experts look at videos of usability tests, give automated feedback on designs, change and get better over time, and help make datasets for UX evaluation. Fan et al. say that both synchronous collaborations, which are how humans and AI work together, and asynchronous collaborations with AI, which include explanations, have been shown to support UX analysts' research better and are seen more positively. AI can also give reports on UX problems, with details that testers can use directly or change further if needed.

c. What are the research opportunities to enhance human- AI collaboration in UX design?

Every company should try to make the UX design process better as a top priority. So, looking for ways to make it easier for humans and AI to work together in UX design could help make digital goods and services easier to use and more enjoyable for users. Support that is powered by AI could make UX processes more successful and efficient. On the other hand, Stige et al. say that AI can't understand or use tacit knowledge when creating, which could limit future options. Table 4 shows the ways that humans and AI can work together better in UX design.

The most talked about opportunity is closing the gap between academic study and UX practice to make a difference in the real world. According to Stige et al., to better understand AI in UX, we should combine theories and methods from different fields, look at the most important tasks in UX design, and find areas where more study is needed. Here are some ways to connect UX study from the classroom to real-world use.

AI models will be made to help artists with the parts of their work that they hate the most. The AI models will focus on parts of the UX workflow that could use more AI-powered help, like searching for design ideas, looking at different design options, customizing the design system, and checking for design rule violations.

With AI, designers can come up with new ideas for both the system and the service. They can see where AI can add value for people and make the experience better for them. Yildirim et al., on the other hand, say that the biggest problem with AI design innovation is that it's hard to show that the features are worth the money and will pay for themselves over time.

AI can help businesses be more customer-focused, creative, and quick to come up with new ideas. Authors Verganti et al. say that AI could help find new ideas by looking at very large datasets and finding patterns and insights that people might not understand. Stige et al. agree that this chance comes about when the customer and the designer work together throughout the whole development process, when there is a shared knowledge of the rules and when businesses change their value chain to include people.

By solving complicated problems, AI changes the way standard design work is done. Verganti et al. talk about using problem-solving loops in AI-powered systems. In these systems, an AI engine gathers real-time data from interactions with customers or the ecosystem to help with the planning process. This method is based on data and lets specific solutions for each user be created automatically, without any help from a person. This leads to more efficient and personalized designs. The problem-solving skills of AI, like being able to recognize objects, understand natural language, make predictions, and come to conclusions, help it make good design choices. New data is constantly being collected, and AI engines in AI-powered systems can learn from this data. This iterative process speeds up the rate of innovation and helps people come up with better ideas.

In addition, privacy protections are put in place during the data collection process. Limiting the collection of personal data to just a few dimensions of information can help protect privacy during the data collection process. This way, sensitive data is not taken for no reason. Encrypting data and using safe storage methods can protect collected data from being accessed or breached by people who aren't supposed to, protecting user privacy and security. Abbas et al. found that these help customers make smart choices about sharing their information, which makes the UX process better.

d. What approaches are used in the Literature to investigate the relationship between AI and the UX process?

Different research methods have been used to look into the connection between AI and UX design, each shedding light on a different part of this complex relationship. One piece of literature looks at UX using frameworks like the AIAD design framework, and one study looks at how AI can be used to automate the design process. For example, Yang et al., who study mobile apps, use user data to rate UX, which helps designers figure out if they need to make iterative design changes. Even though this method could be used to simulate UX and make things run more smoothly, Karimi et al. found that it doesn't do much to improve learning or usefulness, which suggests that deep learning shouldn't be used during the evaluation process. In fact, Lu et al. stress how important it is to include end users directly in the design review process. They do this by using qualitative methods like user testing and walkthroughs to see if user needs have been met, which produces useful qualitative data.

Verganti et al. also talk about how AI has the potential to change things by making solutions that are highly user-centered, creative, and always changing throughout a product's life cycle. This shows how AI can improve UX by providing customized and flexible options.

Fan et al. showed a unique strategy that uses a Hybrid Wizard-of-Oz approach. This method combines controlled user studies, data-gathering tools like surveys and interviews, and AI to fully understand the user's point of view. Some studies also use qualitative methods along with user testing to look at comments from users and find patterns through AI analysis. Notably, automatic methods for measuring how people react to designs have been suggested as a possible replacement for traditional user testing, which would save money.

On the other hand, Wallach et al. argue against the idea that automatic methods should completely take the place of usability testing. They say that usability testing is still necessary to find problems and hurdles, which is important for judging user experience. It becomes clear that a hybrid method that combines AI skills with human design knowledge is likely to produce the best results. When predictive AI models and standard user testing are used together, they can give useful information that goes beyond the limits of either method.

The different methods talked about together help us get a better sense of how AI can improve and shape user experiences in a world where design processes are always changing. The research includes both quantitative and qualitative user participation, pushing for a broad and flexible method to use the best of what AI and human design expertise can do together.

e. What are the gaps in the literature regarding AI for UX design?

After the carefully planned literature review was done, several problems were found in the available literature that related to each research question. In the context of AI for UX design, these gaps help researchers figure out which areas need more information and set them as a top goal.

a. **Lack of understanding of how to effectively work with AI**: Designers are currently not fully capitalizing on the potential of AI, a technology that, despite not being entirely new, harbors considerable promise for the future of AI mediation. The course of AI development appears to be more shaped by the availability of data and the performance of learning systems than by a meticulously crafted, user-centric vision. At present, AI technology is only sparingly integrated into conventional practices of user experience design and notably absent from design patterns, prototype tools, and design education. Yang et al observed a deficiency in comprehension among UX designers concerning deep neural networks.

According to Buschek et al., there isn't a lot of information about designers' personal experiences and views on AI tools. This means that it's hard to understand the problems, successes, and subtleties that designers meet on a daily basis when they work with AI. To make AI tools better fit the needs of designers, we need to learn more about these practical factors.

b. **Gaps in understanding AI limitations in current literature**: The existing literature research on the application AI in UX design highlights several shortcomings. Firstly, there is a scarcity of available tools and materials that support UX-driven ideation utilizing pre-trained models. This limitation impedes designers' ability to make well-informed decisions regarding the seamless integration of AI into their design processes. Moreover, contemporary AI systems primarily focus on graphical interface elements, neglecting crucial design activities that involve a more profound application of "design thinking," such as user interviews and testing.

In addition to these problems, Lu et al.'s study shows that UX professionals also have trouble explaining AI ideas clearly. Even though using AI models could help UX experts communicate better with technical stakeholders, it's hard for them to get these ideas across, which stops AI from being widely used and successfully implemented in UX design. So, fixing these problems with resources and communication plans is necessary to get the most out of AI's ability to make the user experience better.

c. **Methods of evaluating in the literature of AI for UX design**: The primary gap in AI for UX design evaluation methods lies in the limited utilization of literature reviews to identify studies that have explored UX. Many existing studies predominantly rely on participant interviews and design workshops to collect information from designers. Consequently, incorporating review articles and qualitative research methodologies into the evaluation of AI for UX design could facilitate a more thorough analysis. For example, researchers have employed the Wizard of Oz and AIAD scheme to enhance support for UX evaluators' analysis. Additionally, the integration of a data collection function within the software has been developed and implemented, to further enhance the evaluation process. By incorporating these methodologies, a more comprehensive understanding of the effectiveness of AI in UX design can be achieved.

d. **Collaboration**: A collaboration between UX designers and data scientists in AI teams is often challenging due to a gap between their practices and perspectives. Yildirim et al discovered that this gap can lead to a lack of shared workflow and a common language, hindering effective collaboration throughout the AI lifecycle.

However, UX designers need to make AI behavior understandable for users which enables designers to understand why and how AI tools propose certain solutions and improve user experience.

f. How to close the challenge gap in terms of AI support for the UX process?

Every part of the UX process should be improved by looking at how to fill in the holes. Table 5 shows what a number of pieces of writing say is the best way to close the gaps.

There is written material that talks about how to get past not knowing how to work with AI effectively. According to Stige et al., it's important for everyone involved in AI creation to have a full understanding of the whole process and how it affects collaboration between different groups. On the one hand, Bauer and Vocke say that people should learn how to use technology. They should not only try to figure out how AI works, but they should also use works of teamwork and communication, like wireframes and whiteboard sketches, to help them talk to each other.

To understand AI's limits, Stige et al. suggest doing in-depth research and analysis to learn more about its problems and limitations, learning new things all the time, and keeping up with the latest AI developments and research. To get a better understanding of AI's limits, they also suggest that researchers, practitioners, and policymakers work together across disciplines to create a complete picture of these limits and come up with ways to reduce potential risk.

Also, to make up for the fact that there isn't much written about how to evaluate UX design. Zhang et al. say that this method could be supported by doing a retrospective study with UX professionals to learn about how they do their jobs. To go along with this idea from Stige et al. Do systematic literature reviews to find relevant studies on evaluating UX design, talk to experts to get their thoughts and suggestions on evaluation methods, use citation analysis to find key sources and seminal works on evaluating, and look at grey literature and industry reports to find out about the newest developments and insights in evaluating AI for UX design.

Yildirim et al. say that the gap in collaboration between UX designers and data scientists can be closed by encouraging open communication and teamwork to share knowledge and understand each other's points of view, coming up with a common language and set of ideas, and holding training sessions and workshops to help both UX designers and data scientists better understand UX principles and data science ideas. In fact, creators need to make it easy for people to understand how AI works. This hole can be filled by creating AI systems that allow design systems to be customized. The idea that using speech or other nuanced forms of communication can help people understand how complex AI works is supported by Holmquist.

Constraints and Future Work

There are some problems with the literature study that looks at how AI tools can help with UX design. Firstly, the review only looks at 11 papers, which is a small sample compared to the large amount of research on user experience processes. This limitation comes from not having enough time or money, not being able to read certain papers, and the rules set out in systematic literature reviews. Notably, some of the articles that are part of both this review and systematic literature reviews are the same.

Also, the keywords you choose might make it harder to find articles that are useful. In the future, researchers should add more words to the search list so that it includes more synonyms and variations on the theme.

Another important limitation comes from previous study, which shows that we don't fully understand how to use AI as a design material in UX design. This lack of sufficiency leads to wrong results and limited use in modeling. It is suggested that more samples and participants be used during the training and data-collection steps to improve the prediction model. Also, methods must be rigorously validated, which requires larger instance scopes.

Lastly, the chapter tries to be fair while still recognizing how author bias can affect how results are interpreted and how research is designed. Subjectivity could come from the authors' experiences and views, which could affect the study topics, data collection, and analysis without them meaning to. Even when people try to be objective, biases still happen, which shows how important it is for readers to be aware of them. Different points of view and peer review should be used in the investigation to reduce bias, and it is suggested that future studies keep getting better.

Conclusion

AI is now a well-known tool that has an effect on UX design. AI services are being used by professionals in more and more areas of their work, which is changing how they do user research, UI design, and UX review. This chapter talks about how AI helps UX professionals, with a focus on study, evaluation, and design. It talks about the idea of "artificial design intelligence" (ADI) and its benefits, such as making things more efficient, creative, and able to predict trends and come up with design solutions. But problems are also talked about, such as the fact that UX designers and data scientists need to work together, AI modeling doesn't have enough tools and skills, there are risks, and designers are worried about losing their jobs. A review of eleven publications is used as part of the chapter's approach. This gives future UX designers and researchers useful information. The study answers six research questions and looks at academic material to give a full picture of the research problem.

To start, ask the question to learn about and understand the most common problems that come up during the UX process. There are two problems that the discovery brings up: the product and the design and control method. These results show that problems with design choices and not having enough control and freedom in the UX process are common in the field of user UX design. The next question is about how AI is being used to help or improve the UX design process. This shows that normal designing tasks benefit the most from AI technologies compared to analyzing and evaluating users and context.

On the other hand, different studies have shown that new AI systems and services can help people and AI work together better in UX design. The goal of these studies is to find ways that AI can improve people's experiences and make all users happier. However, Yildirim et al. point out that the biggest problem with developing AI design innovation is showing how adding AI features will make money and give a good return on investment.

Third, different methods have been used in the past to study the connection between AI and the UX process. Studies rate UX using frameworks like AIAD, use user data to make changes over time, and stress the importance of involving end users directly through qualitative methods. AI is seen as a game-changer because it creates solutions that focus on the person. A Wizard of Oz-style hybrid method combines data collection, user studies, and AI. Some people suggest using automated methods to track how users react, while others say that the best insights come from a mix of AI and human design knowledge.

Lastly, the challenge gaps are looked at and a plan for how to fix them is given. Some common gaps are not knowing how to work with AI successfully, how UX designers and data scientists should work together, and how designers should make AI behavior easy for users to understand. These problems could be solved by having a full knowledge of the whole process of making AI and how it affects working together between different groups. Promoting open communication and teamwork to help people share information and see things from each other's points of view, and creating AI systems that help with customizing design systems.

References

D. Norman, The Design of Everyday Things. Constellation, 2013.

V. Silva-Rodriguez, S. E. Nava-Munoz, L. A. Castro, F. E. Martinez- Perez, H. G. Perez-Gonzalez, and F. Torres-Reyes, "Classifying designlevel requirements using machine learning for a recommender of interaction design patterns," IETSoftware, vol. 14, no. 5, pp. 544-552, Oct. 2020, doi: 10.1049/iet-sen.2019.0291.

K. Baxter, C. Courage, and K. Caine, Understanding Your Users. Morgan Kaufmann, 2015.

A. Stige, E. D. Zamani, P. Mikalef, and Y. Zhu, "Artificial intelligence (AI) for user experience (UX) design: a systematic literature review and future research agenda," Information Technology & People, Aug. 2023, doi: 10.1108/itp-07-2022-0519.

Y. Lu, C. Zhang, I. Zhang, and T. J.-J. Li, "Bridging the Gap Between UX Practitioners' Work Practices and AI-Enabled Design Support Tools," CHI Conference on Human Factors in Computing Systems Extended Abstracts, Apr. 2022, Published, doi: 10.1145/3491101.3519809.

A. M. H. Abbas, K. I. Ghauth, and C.-Y. Ting, "User Experience Design Using Machine Learning: A Systematic Review," IEEE Access, vol. 10, pp. 51501-51514, 2022, doi: 10.1109/access.2022.3173289.

L. Chen et al., "An artificial intelligence-based data-driven approach for design ideation," Journal of Visual Communication and Image Representation, vol. 61, pp. 10-22, May 2019, doi: 10.1016/j.jvcir.2019.02.009.

O. Nikiforova, V. Zabiniako, J. Kornienko, M. Gasparovica-AsTte, and A. Silina, "Mapping of Source and Target Data for Application to Machine Learning Driven Discovery of IS Usability Problems," Applied Computer Systems, vol. 26, no. 1, pp. 22-30, May 2021, doi: 10.2478/acss-2021-0003.

L. E. Holmquist, "Intelligence on tap," Interactions, vol. 24, no. 4, pp. 28-33, Jun. 2017, doi: 10.1145/3085571.

Q. Yang, A. Scuito, J. Zimmerman, J. Forlizzi, and A. Steinfeld, "Investigating How Experienced UX Designers Effectively Work with Machine Learning," Proceedings of the 2018 Designing Interactive Systems Conference, Jun. 2018, doi: 10.1145/3196709.3196730.

Q. V. Liao, H. Subramonyam, J. Wang, and J. Wortman Vaughan, "Designerly Understanding: Information Needs for Model Transparency to Support Design Ideation for AI-Powered User Experience," Proceedings of the 2023 CHI Conference on Human Factors in Computing Systems, Apr. 2023, Published, doi: 10.1145/3544548.3580652.

O. Nikiforova, V. Zabiniako, J. Kornienko, M. Gasparovica-AsTte, and A. Silina, "Mapping of Source and Target Data for Application to Machine Learning Driven Discovery of IS Usability Problems," Applied Computer Systems, vol. 26, no. 1, pp. 22-30, May 2021, doi: 10.2478/acss-2021-0003.

N. Yildirim et al., "How Experienced Designers of Enterprise Applications Engage AI as a Design Material," CHI Conference on Human Factors in Computing Systems, Apr. 2022, doi: 10.1145/3491102.3517491.

Q. Yang, A. Steinfeld, C. Rose, and J. Zimmerman, "Re-examining Whether, Why, and How Human-AI Interaction Is Uniquely Difficult to Design," Proceedings of the 2020 CHI Conference on Human Factors in Computing Systems, Apr. 2020, doi: 10.1145/3313831.3376301.

Gaffney, G. (2017). The Revolution Will Not Be Handheld. Journal of Usability Studies, 12(3), 92-94.

Koch, J., and Paris-Saclay, I., 2017, "Design Implications for Designing with a Collaborative AI," AAAI Spring Symposium Series., Palo Alto, CA, Mar. 27-29.

N. Voil, User Experience Foundations. BCS, The Chartered Institute for IT, 2019.

R. Verganti, L. Vendraminelli, and M. Iansiti, "Innovation and Design in the Age of Artificial Intelligence," Journal of Product Innovation Management, vol. 37, no. 3, pp. 212-227, Apr. 2020, doi: 10.1111/jpim.12523.

A. Schmidt and A. Etches, Useful, Usable, Desirable. ALA Editions, 2014.

C. Wilson, Interview Techniques for UX Practitioners: A UserCentered Design Method. 2013.

V. P. S. Pandian, "BlackBox Toolkit: Intelligent Assistance to UI Design," arXiv.org, Apr. 04, 2020. https://arxiv.org/abs/2004.01949

S. Li, "The Trend and Characteristic of AI in Art Design," Journal of Physics: Conference Series, vol. 1624, no. 5, p. 052028, Oct. 2020, doi: 10.1088/1742-6596/1624/5/052028.

G. Dove, K. Halskov, J. Forlizzi, and J. Zimmerman, "UX Design Innovation," Proceedings of the 2017 CHI Conference on Human Factors in Computing Systems, May 2017, doi: 10.1145/3025453.3025739.

K. J. K. Feng, M. J. Coppock, and D. W. McDonald, "How Do UX Practitioners Communicate AI as a Design Material? Artifacts, Conceptions, and Propositions," Proceedings of the 2023 ACM Designing Interactive Systems Conference, Jul. 2023, doi: 10.1145/3563657.3596101.

Q. V. Liao, H. Subramonyam, J. Wang, and J. Wortman Vaughan, "Designerly Understanding: Information Needs for Model Transparency to Support Design Ideation for AI-Powered User Experience," Proceedings of the 2023 CHI Conference on Human Factors in Computing Systems, Apr. 2023, doi: 10.1145/3544548.3580652.

D. Satterfield and T. D. Abel, "AI Is the New UX: Emerging Research Innovations in AI, User Experience, and Design as They Apply to Industry, Business, and Education, and Ethics," Advances in Intelligent Systems and Computing, pp. 182-188, 2020, doi: 10.1007/978-3-030-51057-2_26.

Wei, Xu," AI in HCI Design and User Experience," arXiv.org, Feb. 18, 2023. https://arxiv.org/abs/2301.00987

S. Amershi et al., "Guidelines for Human-AI Interaction," Proceedings of the 2019 CHI Conference on Human Factors in Computing Systems, May 2019, doi: 10.1145/3290605.3300233.

Q. Yang, J. Zimmerman, A. Steinfeld, and A. Tomasic, "Planning Adaptive Mobile Experiences When Wireframing," Proceedings of the 2016 ACM Conference on Designing Interactive Systems, Jun. 2016, doi: 10.1145/2901790.2901858.

M. Virvou, "Artificial Intelligence and User Experience in reciprocity: Contributions and state of the art," Intelligent Decision Technologies, vol. 17, no. 1, pp. 73-125, Apr. 2023, doi: 10.3233/idt-230092.

D. Spallazzo, M. Scianname, and M. Ceconello, "Towards a UX Assessment Method for AI-Enabled Domestic Devices," Distributed, Ambient and Pervasive Interactions, pp. 336-347, 2020, doi: 10.1007/978-3-030-50344-4_24.

E. Kuang, "Crafting Human-AI Collaborative Analysis for User Experience Evaluation," Extended A bstracts of the 2023 CHI Conference on Human Factors in Computing Systems, Apr. 2023, doi: 10.1145/3544549.3577042.

M. D. Ekstrand, F. M. Harper, M. C. Willemsen, and J. A. Konstan, "User perception of differences in recommender algorithms," Proceedings of the 8th ACM Conference on Recommender systems, Oct. 2014, doi: 10.1145/2645710.2645737.

M. C. Willemsen, M. P Graus, and B. P Knijnenburg, "Understanding the role of latent feature diversification on choice difficulty and satisfaction," User Modeling and User-Adapted Interaction, vol. 26, no. 4, pp. 347-389, Sep. 2016, doi: 10.1007/s11257-016-9178-6.

L. Micol Policarpo et al., "Machine learning through the lens of ecommerce initiatives: An up-to-date systematic literature review," Computer Science Review, vol. 41, p. 100414, Aug. 2021, doi: 10.1016/j.cosrev.2021.100414.

Y. Jiang et al., "Computational Approaches for Understanding, Generating, and Adapting User Interfaces," CHI Conference on Human Factors in Computing Systems Extended Abstracts, Apr. 2022, Published, doi: 10.1145/3491101.3504030.

H. Snyder, "Literature review as a research methodology: An overview and guidelines," Journal of Business Research, vol. 104, pp. 333-339, Nov. 2019, doi: 10.1016/j.jbusres.2019.07.039.

B. Kitchenham, 'Procedures for performing systematic reviews', Keele University,UK and National ICT Australia, vol. 33, 2004.

J. Franklin, "The Importance of Peer Reviewing," The Scientific World JOURNAL, vol. 1, pp. 23-24, 2000, doi: 10.1100/tsw.2000.18.

D. Buschek, C. Anlauff, and F. Lachner, "Paper2Wire - A Case Study of User-Centred Development of Machine Learning Tools for UX Designers," i-com, vol. 20, no. 1, pp. 19-32, Apr. 2021, doi: 10.1515/icom-2021-0002.

W. Bauer and C. Vocke, "Work in the Age of Artificial Intelligence - Challenges and Potentials for the Design of New Forms of HumanMachine Interaction," Advances in Intelligent Systems and Computing, pp. 493-501, Jun. 2019, doi: 10.1007/978-3-030-20154-8_45.

B. Yang, L. Wei, and Z. Pu, "Measuring and Improving User Experience Through Artificial Intelligence-Aided Design," Frontiers in Psychology, vol. 11, Nov. 2020, doi: 10.3389/fpsyg.2020.595374.

M. Fan, X. Yang, T. Yu, Q. V. Liao, and J. Zhao, "Human-AI Collaboration for UX Evaluation: Effects of Explanation and Synchronization," Proceedings of the ACM on Human-Computer Interaction, vol. 6, no. CSCW1, pp. 1-32, Mar. 2022, doi: 10.1145/3512943.

N. Choudhury, "Can Artificial Intelligence be Used to Improve Productivity by Automating Elements of the User Experience Design Processes?" Jul 2023, Published, doi: 10.20944/preprints202202.0057.v2.

G. Pandey, D. Bhasin, P. Thakur, S. Gonge, R. Joshi, and K. Kotecha, "Obsessive UX: Role of UX & Heuristic Evaluation in Building A Product that Attracts Human Emotions," 2023 IEEE 8th International Conference for Convergence in Technology (I2CT), Apr. 2023, Published, doi: 10.1109/i2ct57861.2023.10126483.

S. Gupta, "An Analysis of UI/UX Designing with Software Prototyping Tools," Advances in Systems Analysis, Software Engineering, and High-Performance Computing, pp. 134-145, 2020, doi: 10.4018/978- 1-5225-9659-2.ch008.

G. A. Boy, Ed., "The Handbook of Human-Machine Interaction," Nov. 2017, Published, doi: 10.1201/9781315557380.

K. E. Weil, "PORTER, Competitive advantage, creating and sustaining superior performance," Revista de Administra^ao de Empresas, vol. 25, no. 2, pp. 82-84, Jun. 1985, doi: 10.1590/s0034-75901985000200009.

D. P. Wallach, L. A. Flohr, and A. Kaltenhauser, "Beyond the Buzzwords: On the Perspective of AI in UX and Vice Versa," Artificial Intelligence in HCI, pp. 146-166, 2020, doi: 10.1007/978-3-030-50334-5_10.

P. Karimi, K. Grace, M. L. Maher, and N. Davis, 'Evaluating creativity in computational co-creative systems', 2018, doi: 10.48550/ARXIV.1807.09886.

Chapter 3
Design Thinking in the Age of AI: Startup Ecosystem Insights

Introduction

Design thinking (DT) has spread like wildfire as a way to come up with new ideas. It has an effect on the culture of organizations, how businesses interact with customers, and the basic ideas that make up the innovation process.

DT was created in the United States when Stanford University and the design consulting firm IDEO joined forces. The goal was to create a space where managers could better understand how designers "reason" in their work flow and where designers could better align their creativity with business and competitive rules.

Even though there isn't a unanimous agreement, existing literature in the field of Innovation Management has pointed out different founding concepts of DT. First, it was pointed out that abductive thinking is a different pattern that is very different from both deduction and induction. The trend here is to use "what-if" and heuristics to come up with new hypotheses that fit the problem context and challenge the current paradigms. A different way to approach innovation is needed to get around the problems with the old "stage-gate" process. This can be done through rounds of iteration, the Human-Centered approach, "framing and reframing" of the problem-context, the constant interaction between the "problem-space" and the "solution-space," and the fact that the problem is usually not clear.

At the moment, though, even though things are getting more stable, only a few changing factors—mostly the arrival of disruptive technologies—are having a big effect on how businesses run and use innovation practices and approaches, such as DT. Disruptive technologies like AI, machine learning, and big data analytics are making not only customer relationship management and marketing better, but also research and development (R&D) and the management of innovation processes as a whole.

In the context of AI, this usually means that a machine can do cognitive tasks like a human mind would, like understanding, reasoning, learning, interacting with its surroundings, fixing problems, and even being creative. Robotics, computer vision, language processing, and machine learning are all tools that AI can use to solve business problems. AI is a technology that can be used for more than one thing. In fact, its field mostly includes a lot of different methods and even different ways of doing things to help different parts of businesses in a lot of different industries. In the financial and banking industries, chatbots and virtual assistants are becoming more common to help people with simple chores as well as more complicated ones like allocating assets and managing their wealth. Also, AI is helping customer relationship management and sales management become more efficient and better understand how users behave and what their problems are.

Which brings up the question of how AI can help DT. What specific role does this technology play in helping businesses innovate in ways that are driven by DT? Also, which parts of DT (which is meant to be a method to innovation that can be used in many industries) are most benefiting from AI solutions? These questions can help us better understand the near future of DT and how creativity, which has long been thought of as a human brain activity that can't be copied, will be improved, harmed, or limited by this new technology. Looking at DT through the lens of its main stages based on previous research and finding new AI services and software that can be used for one or more DT stages is what this chapter is all about. The goal is to help you understand better how disruptive technologies are currently shaking up the DT approach in big or small ways. To give a structured answer to these research questions, this chapter suggests a qualitative analysis of a sample of the most well-funded startups that offer services and tools where AI is used in certain stages or throughout the entire DT process. These startups are seen as a way to predict the next changes in creative approaches and innovation practices.

The chapter is mostly split into four parts: the theoretical background looks at the existing research on DT and chooses the model that will be used for analysis; the research design and case analysis describe the startup sample that was used and how it was analyzed; the findings describe the chapter's original contribution by showing how AI is changing DT; and finally, the conclusions show what the findings mean for the future of DT as a whole.

Theoretical Background

Design Thinking

As one of the first people to try to create a new field that combined innovation and design, Brown (2009) described DT as "a discipline that uses the designer's sensibility and methods to match people's needs with what is technologically possible and what a viable business strategy can turn into customer value and market opportunity." In the words of Micheli et al. (2019), this definition makes DT both a process and a personal trait, or a certain "sensibility" that connects design with business problems. On the other hand, Lockwood says that DT is "a human-centered innovation process that emphasizes observation, collaboration, fast learning, visualization of ideas, rapid concept prototyping, and concurrent business analysis." This shows how the work process of professional designers can be used to solve business problems. Today, the process led by DT has nothing to do with products, processes, or business models. Its scope and results are the same. New ideas also see DT as a way to change the culture of a company by using various tools and methods all the time. This idea is based on the idea of "experiential learning."

A few years ago, experts pointed out a difference between how the process was supposedly modeled in theory and how it was actually carried out. But now, everyone agrees on what the main features and ideas of DT are. Key principles, tools, and constructs have been found through a study that combined a thorough literature review of the most important scientific journals in design and management with a card sorting activity led by design pros. Putting aside the results of DT practice, which are mostly seen as "creativity and innovation" and "problem-solving," ideas like "user-centeredness and involvement," "iteration and experimentation," "interdisciplinary collaboration," "ability to visualize," "holistic view," "abductive reasoning," and "tolerance for ambiguity and failure" are what make DT what it is as a discipline and as a practice. These features make the earlier picture of DT as a "double diamond" more complicated. In that picture, the key stages were thought to be "discover, define, develop, and deliver." In this chapter, the more detailed process articulation created by Micheli et al. (2019) is used to show how AI solutions can be used in DT practices. This helps to identify the following important steps:

- team building and task management, considered as a propaedeutic phase directed to arrange and involve employees from different departments and project stakeholders forming crossdisciplinary teams for the accomplishment of the creative activity;

- sensing and empathizing, where user analysis is run according to the different techniques of user observation, ethnographic research, shadowing and interviews, further collecting information and insights on the problem context and developing "empathy" with the user;
- interpreting andframing, where the design problem is bordered, framed and alternative views and insights are sought for achieving a problem reframing;
- ideating and conceiving, where multiple ideas are proposed to widen the solution space;
- prototyping and learning, to create tangible mock-ups or even probes to be tested to collect feedback and learning for triggering later iterations and refinements;
- launching and measuring, oriented to create an early market for the solution thus measuring with contextual KPIs the early stage performing dynamics.

In DT, cross-disciplinary teams are in charge of building teams and giving out tasks. Research that has been widely read says that cultural diversity and the different points of view that exist in a company can help with innovation and creativity. These ideas seem to be closely linked to the literature on innovation management that talks about how different cultures and fields of study are important for the innovation process.

Sensing and empathizing can be seen as activities that start an innovation project. In this type of work, creative teams try to understand the features and limits of the problem space by building empathy with users and involving them directly in a variety of activities, from passive observation to active participation in co-design. There is a lot of research in the field of innovation management that looks at the different types of engagement and how user involvement affects the results of innovations. This part seems to be connected to that research.

Ideation and conception are at the heart of DT. Brainstorming sessions are mixed with more organized ways to come up with ideas, such as playing metaphorical games or drawing together. At this point, sketching and visualizing seem important because they help with "creative discovery" and allow for reflection and conversation that can help with making decisions.

Sketched ideas turn into mock-ups or probes during the prototyping and learning phase, which is marked by sprint-like approaches and rough modeling techniques. These are becoming more common in businesses thanks to ad hoc digital settings and 3D manufacturing systems that help make digital apps and early releases of physical goods.

Finally, before starting a new round of iterations, the new product, service, or business model needs to be launched for the first time in an early market or with lead users so that the basic KPIs can be tracked. In this way, DT is closely linked to the field of lean entrepreneurship, where the mix of hypotheses and assumptions that support new ideas about products, services, or business models need to be tested to find new ways to make them better. Given the topic of the chapter, the way it was put together helps to show a more complete framework in which new software and services can be connected.

Understanding AI's Evolution: Disruption in the Technology Domain

Scholars and scientists like Herbert Simon, John McCarthy, Claude Shannon, and Nathaniel Rochester took part in a congress in 1956 that talked about the power of calculators and the specific uses of intelligent systems. This congress happened during a time of scientific ferment in the 1930s and 1950s. McCulloch and Pitts's 1943 idea to use computer models to simulate intelligence and the way neural networks work sparked a huge interest in intelligent systems. After some time, in 1950, Alan Turing wrote an article for Mind, an important academic journal that deals with philosophy and psychology, called "Computing machinery and intelligence." In it, he came up with the famous Turing test, which says that a machine is "intelligent" if humans can't tell the difference between its behavior and that of humans.

Starting from that point on, some uses involving math logic and neural networks did very well. The field of AI got a lot of attention, and after a while, it was split into two main categories: "strong AI" and "weak AI." The first theory says that machines can do things and make decisions while being aware of what they're doing. The second theory says that machines can make decisions (like when they play chess) without being aware of what they're doing. As time has gone on, the weak paradigm has gotten the most attention, which has strengthened the idea that robots will never be able to copy the way the brain works.

AI's Main Application Fields

Looking at the current applications of AI algorithms, five classes of solutions - mostly connected to R&D, innovation processes and organizational learning - have been taxonomized:

- intelligent data processing, in this category solutions that deal with structured and unstructured data to extract information from raw data and take action on this basis can be found; here applications can include "pattern discovery", where framing and connections between different types of raw data are established, and "predictive analysis", where applications analyze data to forecast future events or phenomena;

- virtual assistant/chatbot, in this category software agents that can execute commands or accomplish requests through natural language interactions are included;
- recommendation, solutions oriented to guide user preferences and choices on the basis of information provided (as for instance platforms that suggest the purchase of a specific product or propose new movies to watch on the basis of the ones already watched);
- image processing, solutions where single images or videos are analyzed in order to extract precise information;
- language processing, in this category solutions that elaborate languages with the goal of content comprehension, translation, or the autonomous creation of documents using data or other documents as inputs are recognized.

All of the above types of methods could be used for certain parts of the DT process or for the whole thing. For example, an AI pattern discovery app can help a lot with understanding the problem space, and an image processing app can help with analyzing competing products. Language processing software can also help with observing and analyzing users, making it easier for the creative team to save transcripts, match them to different users, and show where parts of the transcript overlap and where they don't.

In both the real world and the literature, we still don't talk about how many AI apps are already in DT or what effect they have. This is the gap in the research on how DT and AI work together that this chapter tries to partially fill. This is what led to the idea of an exploratory study focusing on startups that provide AI-based services for DT, which is what this chapter proposes.

Research Design

The Essentials of Sampling and Skimming

Because there wasn't enough written on the subject, a case study-based experimental study was conducted. The investigation was done on companies that use AI to provide DT services.

It has more than 500,000 records about new businesses, accelerators, and investors. Crunch base® chose the startups. A first skimming process was done on this set of data using major tags that are directly or indirectly linked to DT. This gave us a first sample of 4266 startups. We then quickly went through the descriptions of the tasks that these startups do and chose about 2,100 that were most closely related to DT.

So, an in-depth study was done to get a sample that is easier to work with. Finally, 494 startups have been chosen. Of these, 168 are directly linked to DT and 80 use AI to provide their services and apps. To do the final qualitative case study, we chose the 20 projects that had raised the most money from these 80.

Case Analysis

There were two steps taken to look at the whole group of 20 startups.

For the first round, companies were mostly looked at using secondary sources of data, like information found online about their products to figure out what step was covered in the DT process. This research has given us a first look at how the process is changing and helped us figure out which startups might be worth looking into further. Table 1 shows more information about how the start-ups were put into groups.

Table 1. DT phases coverage

	DT phases covered					
Startup name / Phases of DT	Team Building and Task Management	Sensing and Empathizing	Interpreting and Framing	Ideating and Conceiving	Prototyping and Learning	Launching and Measuring
Veritone, Inc.		***				
Applitools					***	
Gamalon, Inc.		***	***			
Sentiance		***				
Eightfold	***		***			
Test.ai					***	
Eigen Tech			***			
Pymetrics	***	***	***			
Fetch.ai			***			
iGenius	***	***	***	***	***	***
HyperAnna		***	***			

B12					***	
Pixoneye		***				
Gooroo	***	***				
Appvance.ai					***	
Daisee		***				
ForwardLane		***	***			
DataRPM Corp		***				
AdMobilize		***				
Iguazio		***	***			

To get a better idea of this first view, 5 startups have been chosen to be looked at in more detail to see how their services relate to and cover the DT process. There were 20 startups that were looked at, and 5 were chosen because they were good examples of a certain group of offerings. One was chosen for Team Building and Task Management, which was covered by 4 of them, one for Sensing and Empathizing, which was covered by 13 of them, one for Interpreting and Framing, which was covered by 9 of them, and one for Prototyping and Learning, which was covered by 5 of them. Lastly, the only company that covers all stages has been added.

This last sample was mostly looked through to find out what the business has to offer, how much or how little the DT process is covered, which steps are covered, what kind of solution is used for DT, and what changes are made to the process. In Table 2, you can see an overview of this study.

Table 2. Details of the 5 most representative startups

	Main categories of analysis				
	General description	**Partial or whole coverage**	**DT phases covered through AI**	**Specific solution**	**Overall changes in DT**
	(What does the start-up offer? To whom?)	*(Is the DT process covered partially or generally by AI?)*	*(What are the single or more phases covered by the start-up?)*	*(What specific solution is provided to address the DT phase/ phases?)*	*(What changes AI is providing to DT?)*

Startup 1 IGenius, https://igenius. ai, founded in 2016	The company uses AI to build a human-friendly relationship between people and data. IGenius works for any business sector and with any type of data (CRM, marketing data, operations) mainly providing AI-based advisors for business intelligence.	Whole coverage	All	Software based on Natural Language Processing, Machine Learning and fast data retrieval.	Access and analysis of data is reinforced and made central throughout the creative process. Insights are provided handling quickly data diversity, providing statistical significance to ideas, scanning econversations to let ideas emerge, tailoring and even measuring stimuli for creativity.
Startup 2 Sentiance, http://www.sentiance.c om, founded in 2012	Sentiance is a data science company turning IOT sensor data into rich insights about people's behavior and real-time context.	Partial coverage	Main: Sensing and Empathizing	Through using Machine Learning and behavioral modeling, users are observed in real-time in their context to learn about temporal routines and behaviors.	Building empathy with users becomes a direct unbiased process, without the intermediate personal interpretation of the observer. The understanding of users becomes much deeper and can happen in real daily situations, also supporting a more objective framing of problems.

Startup 3 HyperAnna, http://www.hyperanna.com, founded in 2016	HyperAnna is an AI powered data analyst capable of analyzing any type of data within seconds by using natural language.	Partial coverage	Main: Interpreting and Framing	The software generates key insights based on statistically relevant analysis, providing actionable insights within seconds to impact business decisions.	Framing and interpreting problems and users' insights, but also access and analysis of data for the discovery phase of the DT process are improved by AI.
Startup 4 Pymetrics, http://pymetrics. com, founded in 2013	The company matches people to jobs, accurately and fairly, by measuring their cognitive, social, and emotional traits.	Partial coverage	Main: Team building and Task management	Customized Machine Learning and neuroscience are used to make the hiring process more efficient, but also to understand people's true talent for theirs and companies' best success.	Creativity and balance inside teams is made scientific and objective: through measuring and matching people cognitive and emotional traits, teams to deliver different types of tasks are enhanced, while time and resources for HR is greatly reduced.
Startup 5 Applitool, http://applitools. com, founded in 2013	Applitools has developed the first cloud-based software testing tool that automatically validates all the visual aspects of any web platform.	Partial coverage	Main: Prototyping and Learning	Through AI powered visual testing, Applitools revolutionizes the ways app and web platforms are tested.	Prototyping is made more efficient. Visual tests for web products become almost perfect for commercialization thanks to AI.

Main Findings and Discussion

The first study of the whole sample didn't reveal many useful insights, but it did help us get a general idea of where and how AI is changing the DT process. This is summed up in Table 3, which looks at the twenty companies in more detail to find out how much coverage there is for each DT phase using the AI-related areas we talked about earlier. This is helpful for finding out not only which parts of DT are changed the most, but also which AI-based apps are testing this area right now. Also, three key points are discussed below that help you understand what the bigger effects will be of adding AI applications, either partially or completely, to the DT process.

Table 3. Low-Medium-High intensity of coverage of the sample analyzed by DT phases and AI applicative domains

	DT phases					
AI applicative domains	Team Building and Task Management	Sensing and Empathizing	Interpreting and Framing	Ideating and Conceiving	Prototyping and Learning	Launching and Measuring
Intelligent Data Processing	Medium intensity of coverage **3 startups** covering this phase/techno logy (Eightfold, Pymetrics, Gooroo)	High intensity of coverage **8 startups** covering this phase/techno logy (Veritone, Inc., Sentiance, IGenius, Pixoneye, Gooroo, ForwardLan e, DataRPM Corporation, Iguazio)	High intensity of coverage **6 startups** covering this phase/techno logy (Gamalon Inc., Fetch. ai, IGenius, HyperAnna, ForwardLan e, Iguazio)	-	Low intensity of coverage **2 startups** covering this phase/ techno logy (B12 Appvance)	
Virtual Assistant/ Chatbot	-	Low intensity of coverage **1 startup** covering this phase/ techno logy (Gamalon, Inc.)	-	-	-	-

Recom-menda-tion	-	Medium intensity of coverage **5 startups** covering this phase/techno logy (Gamalon Inc., Pixoneye, Daisee, ForwardLane, AdMobilize)	Low intensity of coverage **1 startup** covering this phase/techno logy (Gamalon Inc.)	-	-	-
		Low intensity of coverage			Medium intensity of coverage	
Image Process-ing		**1 startup** covering this phase/ techno logy (AdMo-bilize)			**3 startups** covering this phase/ techno logy (Applitools, Test.ai, Ap-pvance)	
Lan-guage Process-ing	-	Low intensity of coverage **1 startup** covering this phase/ techno logy (Daisee)	Low intensity of coverage **1 startup** covering this phase/ techno logy (Eigen Tech-nologies)	-	-	-

The part of the process that AI software currently covers is the research part in DT. This includes both the early stages, when teams are being formed (team building) and problems and user needs are being identified, read, and interpreted (sensing and empathizing, interpreting and framing); and the later stages, when research is mostly used to test and confirm ideas (prototyping and learning). This is clear from both Table 1 and 3. It's interesting to see that most of the AI work is being done on the Sensing and Empathizing stage (Table 3), since at least one of the startups in our sample is suggesting one of the use cases listed to help with innovation in this area. At these stages, AI can help with many jobs that humans used to do mostly. AI is clearly helping with knowledge management and making sense of huge amounts of data in a way that humans might find hard to handle. For example, software can combine different types of datasets and data sources to find statistically significant insights much faster than before. In addition, a lot of the apps in the sample suggest that AI is a better way to look at and understand how people act by using statistics to look at data from places like social networks, different types of websites, sensors put around cities, and apps on phones. This could mean a new era for observing and analyzing users, where AI can add a more scientific and objective element to qualitative analysis, changing a job that was once thought of as a subjective or qualitative part of the design process.

On the other hand, machine-thinking hasn't really hit on a part of DT that has to do with creativity and coming up with new ideas. This is true even though artificial brains can make strange connections by copying the human mind. This part of DT isn't talked about much in our sample, which shows that creative jobs are still the ones that won't be taken over by machines any time soon.

AI is already known for its ability to manage data and knowledge. The analysis shows a new trend that will come about soon based on new types of algorithms that can improve, speed up, and strengthen the hiring process in companies. These algorithms will look at the psychological sides of people to find the "perfect match" that will help collaboration and creativity. This is currently used to improve teamwork and participation within the same group, as well as the way that companies and users work together.

When looking more closely at the smaller sample that was studied, there are a few major findings that can be made about how the DT phases changed.

When it comes to building teams and managing tasks, which are very important parts of DT, AI is making things easier by combining people from different countries and backgrounds based on what neuroscience has shown about people's natural traits and attitudes. In this way, AI supports the idea that creativity is a group effort because it creates the right conditions to begin the process as a connected activity where different inputs from different points of view usually lead to a complete understanding of a design issue.

Sensing and understanding how users feel has always been seen as a key way to come up with new ideas. Because of this, AI is enabling a very important change: it lets businesses and organizations get statistical proof on the emotional side of users by looking at their actions in their natural environment, without any observer or subjective biases. With Sentiance's example of IoT sensors, this is exactly what they do: they collect data and recreate user patterns so that companies and creative teams can understand without any observer or individual bias. The emotional side of design is generally gained through interviews, field research, and direct observations. This is also one of the biggest changes that happened. These terms used to include bias that came from either the situation or the observer's personal view of it. AI is now giving managers and designers access to a lot of less skewed data on how people behave, feel, and react neurologically and psychologically. This changes what it means for a design problem to have an empathic dimension.

By looking at the HyperAnna case, we can see how AI is becoming more useful for data analysis, both to combine data from different sources and to provide statistical proof in situations where it was too expensive to do so before AI. A lot of the work that needs to be done at the start of the DT process is done faster and with less effort. This is especially true when it comes to combining and extrapolating data from different business areas and different sources. This is a great way to get scientifically sound information that can help you come up with new ideas. It speeds up the process, makes it more efficient, and in some cases even makes it automatic. When you scan e-conversations, you can get customized data and analysis. This way, you can use all of your interactions and conversations to come up with business ideas, and you can start the planning process at any time.

Finally, AI is simplifying a lot of the steps needed to make prototypes and learn for the next version. This is still a new idea, and it's mostly used in web apps and platforms where AI-based solutions can test with users and make visual changes instantly. The main reason for these changes is to save money for businesses, since web platforms are an important part of any kind of deal and had to be tested for many hours, even though they might never be perfect. But as AI becomes more popular, it will likely be used to prototype a lot more types of goods and services besides web platforms. For instance, AI could simulate user behaviors and cognitive processes that were previously studied through IoT sensors to run more effective virtual prototyping sessions. Based on the results, AI could then automatically iterate solutions for improvement, removing almost all human involvement from the final part of the DT process. Because of this, prototyping and learning is one of the most interesting stages to keep an eye on, since AI could change it in big ways in the future.

Future Remarks and Conclusions

AI is having many different effects on DT, as shown by the analysis of results. As AI spreads, people will likely pay more attention to the "context of the solution" in the future. Right now, DT is mostly focused on the "context of the (design) problem," and how humans can frame and reframe the design problem doesn't seem to matter much. As a result of AI, the study phase is getting shorter and faster. This is because AI can combine different sources of data, connect them, and process them in a matter of seconds. This is likely to make managers and designers focus more on activities that involve coming up with new ideas and concepts. This means that imagination will be used less for analysis and more for coming up with new solutions, which goes against the DT guiding principles. Additionally, if AI makes it easier for design managers to hire and choose people with a range of mental traits and creative attitudes, their work will focus more on leading the stages of visioning and developing ideas. In other words, they won't be getting direction from above; instead, they will go straight into the creative process with fresh ideas and skills.

Finally, it looks like AI is moving into the prototyping and learning phase, which could lead to a future where robots or "intelligent agents" instead of humans test products and services. Designers test their solutions on virtual people who have real preferences and emotions.

To wrap up, it's important to note that this chapter's attempt to look at the possible future effects of AI on DT through new ideas offered by successful startups is limited by the way it was written. So, a few suggestions are made for future study. First, in-depth direct interviews can be used to get first-hand information that can be added to the case study. This extra task could make the ideas that came from analyzing cases stronger and help find new ones. Second, the analysis of startups could add to the analysis of existing companies that are selling DT-supporting apps and services. It's possible that a study of incumbents would give a more exploitative view, since apps and services are already being sold to different businesses and industries. This study might give a full picture of how AI solutions are being used in DT processes right now.

References

BASSETT-JONES, N. (2005). The paradox of diversity management, creativity and innovation. Creativity and innovation management, 14(2): 169-175.

BECKMAN, S. L., BARRY, M. (2007). Innovation as a learning process: Embedding design thinking. California management review, 50(1): 25-56.

BICHENO, J., HOLWEG, M. (2000). The lean toolbox. Vol. 4. Buckingham: PICSIE books.

BOSCH-SIJTSEMA, P., Bosch, J. (2015). User involvement throughout the innovation process in high-tech industries. Journal of Product Innovation Management, 32(5): 793-807.

BROWN, T. (2009). Change by design. Canada: HarperCollins.

CARLGREN, L., RAUTH, I., ELMQUIST, M. (2016). Framing design thinking: The concept in idea and enactment. Creativity and Innovation Management, 25(1): 38-57.

COOPER, R.G. (1990). Stage-gate systems: a new tool for managing new products. Business horizons, 33(3): 44-54.

COX, T. H., BLAKE, S. (1991). Managing cultural diversity: Implications for organizational competitiveness. Academy of Management Perspectives, 5(3): 45-56.

CROSS, N. (1999). Natural intelligence in design. Design studies 20.1: 25-39.

CROSS, N. (2011). Design thinking: Understanding how designers think and work. Oxford: Bloomsbury.

DELL'ERA, C., VERGANTI, R. (2010). Collaborative strategies in design-intensive industries: knowledge diversity and innovation. Long Range Planning, 43(1): 123-141.

DORST, K., CROSS, N. (2001). Creativity in the design process: co-evolution of problem-solution. Design studies, 22(5): 425-437.

EISENHARDT, K. M. (1989). Building theories from case study research. Academy of management review, 14(4): 532-550.

ELSBACH, K. D., STIGLIANI, I. (2018). Design thinking and organizational culture: A review and framework for future research. Journal of Management, 44(6): 2274-2306.

GIBSON, C. B., GIBBS, J. L. (2006). Unpacking the concept of virtuality: The effects of geographic dispersion, electronic dependence, dynamic structure, and national diversity on team innovation. Administrative Science Quarterly, 51(3): 451-495.

KAVAKLI, M., SCRIVENER, S., BALL, L.J. (1998). Structure in idea sketching behaviour. Design studies, 19(4): 485-517.

KELLEY, T., LITTMAN, J. (2009). The Ten Faces of Innovation: IDEO Strategies for Beating the Devil's Advocate and Driving Creativity Throughout Your Organization. USA: Langara College.

LIEBOWITZ, J. (2001). Knowledge management and its link to artificial intelligence. Expert systems with applications 20.1: 1-6.

LIEDTKA, J., OGILVIE, T. (2011). Designing for growth: A design thinking tool kit for managers. USA: Columbia University Press.

LIEDTKA, J. (2015). Perspective: Linking design thinking with innovation outcomes through cognitive bias reduction. Journal of Product Innovation Management, 32(6): 925-938.

LINSEY, J. S., CLAUSS, E.F., KURTOGLU, T., MURPHY, J.T., WOOD, K.L., MARKMAN, A.B. (2011). An experimental study of group idea generation techniques: understanding the roles of idea representation and viewing methods. Journal of Mechanical Design, 133(3): 1-15.

MAGNUSSON, P. R., MATTHING, J., KRISTENSSON, P. (2003). Managing user involvement in service innovation: Experiments with innovating end users. Journal of Service Research, 6(2): 111124.

MARTIN, R., MARTIN, R.L. (2009). The design of business: Why design thinking is the next competitive advantage. Harvard: Harvard Business Press.

MICHALSKI, R.S., CARBONELL, J.G., and MITCHELL T.M., eds. (2013). Machine learning: An artificial intelligence approach. Springer Science & Business Media.

MICHELI, P., WILNER, S. J., BHATTI, S. H., MURA, M., BEVERLAND, M. B. (2019). Doing Design Thinking: Conceptual Review, Synthesis, and Research Agenda. Journal of Product Innovation Management, 0(0): 1 -25.

MILES, M.B., et al. (1994). Qualitative data analysis: An expanded sourcebook. Sage.

MULLER, R. M., THORING, K. (2012). Design thinking vs. lean startup: A comparison of two user-driven innovation strategies. International Design Management Research Conference, 1-12.

NEMADI, H.R., et al. (2002). Knowledge warehouse: an architectural integration of knowledge management, decision support, artificial intelligence and data warehousing. Decision

Support Systems 33.2: 143-161.

Observatory of Artificial Intelligence Report 2018 - Politecnico di Milano - https://www.osservatori.net/it_it/pubblicazioni?productor_name=499

JEPPESEN, L. B. (2005). User toolkits for innovation: Consumers support each other. Journal of product innovation management, 22(4): 347-362.

SHAH, J. J., VARGAS-HERNANDEZ, N., SUMMERS, J.D., KULKARNI, S. (2001). Collaborative Sketching (C-Sketch)—An idea generation technique for engineering design. The Journal of Creative Behavior, 35(3): 168-198.

SCHELL, C. The value of the case study as a research strategy. Manchester Business School, available at: http://finance-mba.com/Case%20Method.pdf.

SMITH, G. F. (1998). Idea-generation techniques: A formulary of active ingredients. The Journal of Creative Behavior, 32(2): 107-134.

STICKDORN, M., SCHNEIDER, J. (2010). This is Service Design Thinking: Basics, Tools, Cases. The Netherlands: BIS Publisher.

ULRICH, K. T., EPPINGER, S. D. (2003). Product design and development. NY: McGraw-Hill Education.

VAN DER LUGT, R. (2005). How sketching can affect the idea generation process in design group meetings. Design studies, 26(2): 101-122.

VERSTIJNEN, I. M., VAN LEEUWEN, C., GOLDSCHMIDT, G., HAMEL, R., HENNESSEY, J.M. (1998). Sketching and creative discovery. Design studies, 19(4): 519-546.

YIN, R. K. (1981). The case study as a serious research strategy. Knowledge, 3(1): 97-114.

YIN, R. K. (2017). Case study research and applications: Design and methods. USA: Sage publications.

Chapter 4
Systematic Review of AI in UX Design: Current Insights and Future Research

Introduction

When designers make a digital product or service, they have to make sure that the general user experience meets the needs and expectations of the end user. In fact, end users have stopped using things because of bad UX, which has been linked to tech stress, fatigue, and abuse. People who use digital products have high expectations for what they want from an app or service. The success of software is often tied to how well creators can understand those expectations and turn them into features that work well and look good. Following a flexible user-centered design process and being creative, problem-solving, empathetic, and able to work with others are all skills that have been shown to lead to new and useful solutions. It still takes a lot of time, skill, and resources to design something, though. When designers have to figure out both what to make (problem setting) and how to make it (problem solving), their job gets harder. To understand the job at hand, designers need to find out how people will use the solution they've created. This is usually done by looking at data from people who have used the system. Still, there isn't always this kind of info available, which makes the job even harder.

Recently, artificial intelligence (AI) has become popular. This has led to a discussion about how to improve the UX design process by giving creators tools that help them make better digital products in less time and for less money. In the past few years, both study and real-world use of AI for UX have grown quickly. Utilizing data sets that include things like user data or GUI elements allows AI programs to simplify design tasks and make it easier to create adaptive interfaces that change based on changing user needs. Like this, AI-supported UX is completely changing what was possible when it came to making digital things. The field of AI is made up of many subfields, each with its own set of applications and areas of expertise. This means that there are many ways to use data to help or drive UX processes. Still, we don't fully understand how AI has changed and will continue to change UX design at this point. It's very important for the field of Information Systems to look into this new area of study because digital tools work best when they meet specific needs and expectations of users.

It is important to know how AI and other technologies can be created and used in the design process because they have already made big changes to the UX design process. Abbas et al. (2022), in a new literature review, talk about the problems UX designers run into when they try to use machine learning (ML) in their work. The authors list a number of tools, algorithms, and methods that can be used to deal with new problems in their results. In the end, Abbas et al.'s (2022) study adds to the conversation by looking into the main problems UX designers encounter when they try to learn about ML and use it in their work. Still, they don't spend as much time thinking about how ML can be used in the different stages of the UX design process. Some people say that adding new digital tools like AI to the UX design process will significantly alter the way designers do their jobs. Some people say that these kinds of changes can lead to bold new ways of doing news, as well as some bad effects that weren't meant to happen. Some people say that using AI in the UX design process can lead to a lack of control and autonomy, bad UX design, performance losses, and more stress and anger among designers because they are afraid of losing their jobs. Since this is the case, some say that for AI to be useful in UX design, both the technology and human aspects of the process need to be understood. Because of this, it is important to start with the UX design process and figure out how AI is used at each stage.

The goal of this chapter is to look at current academic literature to find out how AI has changed UX design over the past few years and what challenges and opportunities it brings. So, we use a structured literature review method to bring together previous research in order to get a better sense of how and how much AI is changing the design process. Based on this summary, we then look at current study gaps and areas that could be good for future research. So, we make a full study agenda to show the important areas that still need to be studied in terms of how humans and AI can work together in UX design. That is, this study is based on two main research questions:

RQ1: How does AI help or make the UX design process possible right now?

What are some gaps and important study directions that need to be filled right now to improve how humans and AI work together in UX design?

These two research questions are related to our review of the existing literature, as well as our critical evaluation and creation of the research plan. In the next part, we'll talk about some important related work that has to do with defining AI and the design process. We use these two parts to build our systematic literature because they tell us what this chapter is about and what kind of design we'll be focusing on. Part 3 puts together a summary of recent study by mapping out important areas on the design process framework. We look at some important ways AI can be used in the planning process, as well as some worries and problems that come up when using AI. Then, in Section 4, a study agenda is made with specific questions and ideas for future scientific research. Finally, Section 5 talks about the work's theoretical and practical effects and points out some problems.

Background

User Experience (UX) Design Process

Design is the part of creativity that deals with choices and how people come up with new ideas and solve problems. Verganti et al. (2020) say that design practice is "the phenomenology of design in a specific context: its process ("how" design decisions are made; through which phases, methods, tools, or collaborative practices) and the object of design (which design decisions are made; what new solution it creates, whether it's a good, service, or process)". Design principles, on the other hand, are "the perspective and philosophy that inform the act of designing and that make up an ontology of what design is." Yang et al. (2020) say that UX is "an overall experience, which includes all aspects of how users interact with products or services." UX, on the other hand, is "...a person's thoughts and feelings about using or planning to use a product, system, or service, including all of those thoughts, feelings, preferences, perceptions, physical and psychological responses, behaviors, and accomplishments that happen before, during, and after use" (ISO 9241-210:2010). All of these definitions have one thing in common: they all focus on the user and how they interact with the digital solution that was created.

A lot of attention has been paid to the process of creating the UX over the last few years. UX design, according to A. Schmidt and Etches (2014), is "the process of supporting user behavior through usability, usefulness, and desirability provided in the interaction with a product." Following a set and clearly defined method is an important part of designing the UX. Piloting, testing, and improving are all important parts of the process. The goal of user-centered design is to put people who will be using the product at the center of the design and development process. It is a way of creating UX that is often used for digital solutions. Each step of the process can also be linked to a different UX activity, which gives more information about how the process changes when AI is added. According to Preece et al., user-centered design is the process of finding out what the user wants and needs, coming up with ideas, and then judging how well the ideas meet those needs and wants. Iterative design is an important part of user-centered design because the steps can be done again if the end result doesn't meet the needs of the users after each revision. The user-centered design process lets the user and the designer interact in a dynamic way by letting UX designers think about, talk about, and evaluate their design before making the end product.

Figure 1. User centred design and development process.

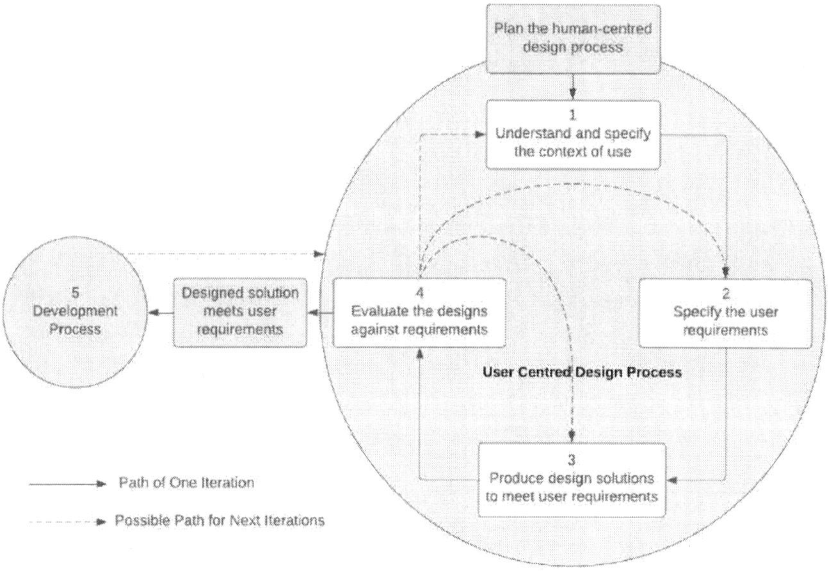

Artificial Intelligence (AI) in Design of UX

AI has been defined in many different ways, but Nilsson (1998) gave the most complete and inclusive explanation by saying that AI is "the study of intelligent behavior in objects." In turn, intelligence behavior includes things like seeing, thinking, learning, talking, and acting in complicated situations. One of the long-term goals of AI is to make machines that can do these things as well as or even better than people... "There is a consensus that AI refers to giving the computer human-like capabilities," which means that computers can do things that usually require human intelligence. This is what Enholm et al. (2021) say about the different definitions of AI. Due to AI's many benefits, as shown by its most recent uses in real life, there is growing interest in how it can be used to improve or even completely change the way digital solutions are designed. In particular, AI has been praised for its many useful features, such as its ability to allow for more customization on a large scale, more accurate research of how digital solutions are used, and support in the creative process for designers.

As the use of AI for design has grown, so have the ideas that are used to explain it. These ideas either explain what AI for design is all about or are used to rate how well AI is doing at things like coming up with new and creative ideas. Artificial design intelligence (ADI) is one of these ideas. This is about AI that has learned about design by using ML to guess what design trends will be and make designs. Computational creativity is another example. This is a branch of AI where computers act in ways that humans would describe as artistic. In the same vein, intelligent design is a subfield that looks at how AI can connect with art design. Artificial intelligence aided design, artificial design intelligence system, user experience design of artificial intelligence products, and artificial intelligence product manager are some of the things that fall under this area. To be fair, there is a lot of potential in using AI in the planning process, but the field is still very mixed. Because of this, it's hard to get a full picture of how AI is currently used in the design process, how it can be improved, and, most importantly, how the rise of AI might completely change the design process as we know it. We do a systematic literature study that builds on this cross-disciplinary area because of this. The goal is to make a map of what is known now and come up with a research agenda for the future that can help both academics and practitioners. In particular, we want to make a contribution to the new field of human-AI collaboration and learn more about how people connect with new AI technologies. AI applications are being used in more and more jobs, including UX design. To get the most out of collaboration, it's important to know how processes and interactions change over time.

Methodology

Following the way suggested by Tranfield et al. (2003), we will now talk about how we plan to do our systematic literature review. As the first step in the planning stage, we came up with our research questions, the main point of the review, our search strategy, and the criteria we would use to include and exclude sources. Then, we went through the first group of papers and got rid of any duplicates or papers that weren't important to our research questions. Finally, we evaluated all the papers that were left in the group based on their quality and how well they answered our research questions. The last step was to look over the papers in the final group. We will talk about these stages in more detail next. Figure 2 shows an outline of how we plan to do things.

Figure 2. Methodology for the systematic literature review

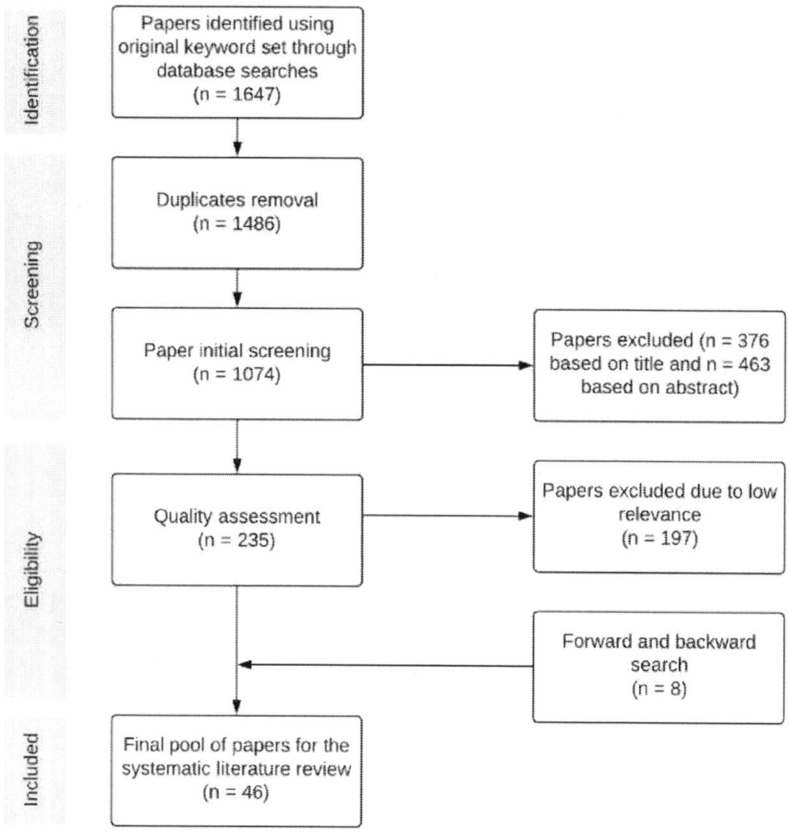

Preparation

During the preparation stage, we made sure our research questions were clear and planned and formalized our search strategy. The first thing we did in this step was a quick review of the existing literature to get a feel for the field and see where there might be gaps in the knowledge when it comes to AI uses in UX and user-centered design studies. This step showed us why we needed to do a systematic study of the current state of the art and helped us find useful keywords for the selection stage.

Selection and screening

We set our guidelines for what to include and what to leave out so that we could find papers that talk about AI as part of user-centered design and UX. Some papers had to be about using AI in the design process, and more specifically, they had to talk about how AI was/could be used to help or replace the work of a designer or front-end developer. These papers weren't about how AI can help end users customize a design solution or how to design AI solutions. As part of our search approach, the studies should also have been:

- Published after 2015;
- The right type of output: journal paper, conference paper, book chapter;
- Published in peer reviewed and reputable journals and conference proceedings.

After doing some preliminary research on the literature, we came up with keywords that fit the focus of our study and the standards for inclusion. You can find these in Table 1.

Table 1. Keywords for the systematic literature review.

Categories	Keywords
AI	Artificial Intelligence, AI, Machine Learning, Deep Learning, Artificial Design Intelligence
Design	User Experience, UX, User Interface, UI, User Customisation, UX Design, Design Prototyping, Human Computer Design, Human Computer Interaction, Co-creation, Intelligent Design, User-centred design, Usability

After that, we started our search on Google Scholar using all possible keyword combos. We decided to use Google Scholar because it has been a useful and simple way to find peer-reviewed studies and reduce publication bias (finding studies that were published in places that aren't always indexed). Along with the given keyword combinations, we also searched in a number of other databases, such as Scopus, the ACM digital library, the AIS library, the IEEE Xplore digital library, and search engines for publishers (such as Taylor and Francis, JSTOR, and Springer). This was to make sure that we had found all the relevant publications. Between October 29, 2022, and November 27, 2022, we searched for and chose the stories. This gave us a total of 1647 articles, which we then put into Zotero, a reference manager program, to make sorting easier.

Screening meant looking at the 1647 papers to see if they met our inclusion standards. We got rid of any papers that weren't peer-reviewed journal articles, conference papers, or book chapters. Some important papers, like doctoral dissertations and reports, were kept in a separate folder. We used these papers to find key facts for the introduction and to help us find good areas for future study, but not for the major synthesis of articles. The titles and abstracts of the studies were also used to sort them. After getting rid of duplicates, screening, and using our guidelines for what to exclude, there were only 38 papers left in the pool. By searching both forward and backward, 8 more pieces were found and added to the group of 46 papers. We noticed that these articles weren't found in our first search because they used specialized or different words to talk about specific AI techniques (like feedforward artificial neural networks) that we didn't have in our list of keywords, or because they didn't talk about any of these in their abstracts or keyword lists.

Quality Assessment

As part of the quality review, we looked at how relevant, rigorous, and trustworthy the papers were. We checked a study's relevance by seeing if it answered our research questions. We also checked a study's relevance by looking at whether it had been reviewed by other researchers and where it was published. Then, we looked at trustworthiness by reading each study carefully and going with what everyone on the team thought. The themes were found independently by two of the co-authors, and then everyone came to an agreement after five study assistants joined the discussion. Because of this evaluation, 38 papers made it into the final group. To make sure we didn't miss any important papers in our search, we looked at the reference lists of all 38 papers that passed quality assessment twice, once going forward and once going backward. There were 8 relevant, rigorous, and trustworthy papers that we found that weren't found during the search process. We added them to our final group of papers. Because of this, 46 studies were looked at in total as part of this systematic literature review.

Data Extraction

To make it easier to get the data, we organized our analysis of the works into a concept matrix. Building on an idea matrix can be helpful because it helps describe the group of papers and put together the results of each part based on the goal of the review. For our concept matrix, we took out the title, the abstract, the main idea, the research question(s), any relevant definitions, the research method used, the main findings and contributions to the field, as well as any limits and steps or avenues for future research. We took Table 2, Table 3, Table 4, and Table 5 straight from this matrix to use in our study of the papers we collected. In a way similar to how the papers were chosen, two of the co-authors used a concept matrix to separately code the papers' contents and themes. Then, these concept maps were put next to each other and talked about with five study assistants. This process helped everyone understand the material and the main ideas that were important.

Data analysis and synthesis

The majority of the papers that were kept for further study came out in 2021 (17 papers) and 2020 (13 papers). Most of these pieces (29 papers) are conference papers, which is how authors who work in UX and user-centered design usually get their work published: in conferences like HCI and ACM SIGCHI. The word cloud in Figure 3 makes it clear that most of the studies are looking into how to use AI and its uses for automation, as well as how to explore and create personas and interfaces and do prototyping in general. After the descriptive analysis, we used the idea matrix to do a qualitative analysis of the articles. We then put together the results along the main areas of user-centered design, which are: context of use; requirements analysis; solution design; design evaluation; and development. Figure 1 shows a framework for user-centered design that these ideas were based on.

Figure 3. Word cloud using the total of keywords used in the identified articles per type of output

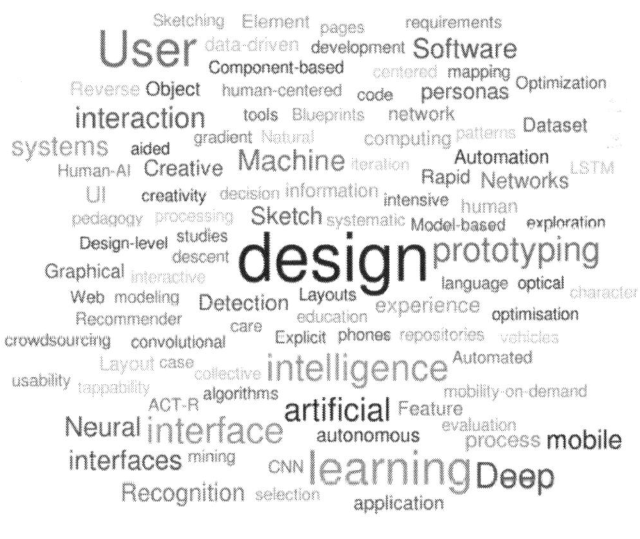

(darker and larger words represent higher frequency in the corpus).

Findings and Analysis

This part talks about the results of our review of the 46 studies we found and focuses on the research questions we asked for our own study. In particular, we look at the current state of the art when it comes to using AI in the digital design process. We also go into more detail about study gaps and important directions for making it easier for humans and AI to work together in UX design. We do this by using the User Centered Design Framework that we talked about earlier. This lets us find and describe AI uses in the different parts of the framework as well as broader uses as part of the process.

AI and the digital design process

Based on our review of the articles we found, AI is mostly used to make the design solution (step 3 in the user-centered design and development process, Figure 1). In fact, 35% of the papers we looked at were about this step. 31% of the articles talk about automatically creating the solution, which is the second most common use of AI (step 5 in the user center design and development process, Figure 1). The rest of the articles are mostly about using AI to evaluate the design solution and automatically figure out how it will be used. As you can see, we didn't find any papers that were specifically about defining requirements.

AI uses for understanding the context of use

While some studies only suggest using AI for certain parts of the design process, others suggest using AI tools and AI-enabled methods to help designers better understand how their digital solutions will be used. We use the phrase "combination of social, physical, task, technical, and information" to describe the things that affect the user experience. It is very important to know the context of use of a digital solution. This means knowing who the intended user is, what their personal context is, how, when, and where they might use the digital solution, and what could be done to make their experience better when interacting with that solution. To get this information, datasets are often used to create user personas or portraits, which are then used to analyze the data. The results are then used to guide low-fidelity prototyping of goods and interfaces. Table 2 shows a summary of studies that look at this part of the design process. These studies suggest using AI tools and methods to automate the parts of the design process that help show a better idea of how the digital solution will be used.

To start, making user personas to learn about the traits of the ideal customer means getting access to relevant datasets. These datasets can help with the creation of personas by providing demographic information and other traits that may be important for certain solutions, such as those used for personalization and recommendation. These kinds of files are often made through market research, and analyzing them can help you get a better sense of what the digital solution needs to support and not support in terms of behaviors and features.

That being said, this way of making user personas can take a lot of time and may require skills that the creator doesn't have. So, Salminen et al. (2019) suggest using machine learning to make this part of the design process automatic by creating characters and profiles on its own. They looked at think-aloud records of interviews with research and marketing experts and came to the conclusion that automating the personas would speed up and improve the accuracy of the results. They also say that personas that are made automatically seem to have the same problems as personas that are made by hand when it comes to usability, perception, credibility, and how they relate to information material. To put it another way, the problems that caused them are not always fixed.

Second, designers often start with low-fidelity prototypes, like sketches, which they use to show off possible solutions and learn more about how a user might interact with the answer. Once the low-fidelity prototype's design is stable, it's time for the designer to add more details and move on to mid-fidelity and high-fidelity prototypes (i.e., UI code that can be run). It can be hard to move between these levels of prototyping, though, because low-fidelity prototypes let users judge digital solutions based on their own personal visions, which will be different for each person, and high-fidelity prototypes don't always clearly show the original idea that was thought up during ideation. After that, there are a lot of changes, which can use up a lot of time and money. Suleri et al. (2019) suggest using deep neural networks to go from low-fidelity to mid-fidelity to high-fidelity prototyping. This lets the stages be switched between automatically and quickly, making the process easier and letting you show how, say, a user interface might look from a rough sketch.

Table 2. AI uses for understanding the context of use.

Source	Research Method	Type of AI and solution	Key findings
Suleri et al. (2019)	Usability evaluation using SUS-schema with 15 designers. Workload analysis using NASA-TLX with 8 participants.	Prototyping workbench where designers can sketch out their ideas. The solution then uses deep neural networks to create a mid-fidelity prototype, and then the executable UI code.	AI can address the frustration designers experience when they need to move from a low fidelity to mid and high fidelity prototypes (as evidenced via the NASA-TLX test). Current tools approach switching from low to mid to high fidelity prototyping as distinct steps, but they are interconnected, and AI can provide comprehensive support.

Salminen et al. (2019)	Eye-tracking user study, using automatically generated persona profiles.	Automatically generated personas (AGP) using online analytics data.	AGP can be developed rapidly and can be behaviourally very accurate; they also enhance communication with the client/organisation.

AI use for user requirements specification

Our search didn't turn up any studies that looked at automating the process of defining user needs. This might be because of the way the requirements specification process works. It usually includes things like role playing, focus groups, and in-depth interviews to get design rules and functional and non-functional requirements for a product.

At the same time, we acknowledge that the main challenge is how a designer can meet the known goals, which lets them know what needs to be made early on in the design process. Along these lines, Koch (2017) says that possibly AI can be used to "[discuss] the stated requirements with the system, which in turn suggests first ideas, similar projects, or inferred information. The system changes what it knows based on the designer's comments and then shows it to the designer to talk about further. So, AI can be used to get important task-related information from the designer through this kind of conversation. This can then help the designer better understand and meet the initial requirements.

AI use for solution design

User-centered design means coming up with ideas that meet the needs of users. Usually, this means using design principles to make prototypes that are changed over and over again to come up with more detailed answers. Table 3 shows a summary of the study that has already been done on using AI for this step in the user-centered design process, that is, for making solutions that meet user needs.

Most of the studies that have been done so far are about how AI can help designers either move from a low-fidelity solution to a high-fidelity solution (e.g., Pandian et al., 2020) or make their ideas better. For instance, O'Donovan et al. (2015) and Duan et al. (2020) both talk about a machine learning method that can change and improve a design on its own. In the business world, Microsoft and Airbnb have also created test programs that use AI to turn sketches on paper into GUI code. But so far, responses to these kinds of methods have been mixed. In particular, these kinds of solutions have been criticized because ML-based ones that turn UI sketches into code suggest that designers will have a lot less control over the end product, which is something designers want and shows that a collaboration between designers and AI would be better.

In fact, some methods put more emphasis on making sure that creators are in charge of the design process by letting them pick the inputs for the AI part. According to one study, AI can make good ideas for optimization based on a sketch made by a designer. This is because the designer is given several options to pick from instead of just one. In addition, scholars mostly agree that AI should not be used for automating the entire process but rather offer to designers the tools that can make the design process easier and more accurate. For example, supervised machine learning can help designers find design trends that make things easier to use, and deep learning can help improve the performance of designs when they are being changed over and over again.

Table 3. Uses of AI for designing solutions

Source	**Research Method**	**Type of AI and solution**	**Key findings**
Duan et al. (2020)	Experiment using 108 different layouts of a photo editing UI	ML is used for updating UI layouts based on designer feedback, task performance, time completion and error rate.	Optimising layouts using ML is time efficient and leads to new ideas, but requires human involvement for refining the solution be aesthetically pleasing. The recommendation is to have a designer-AI collaboration rather than relying on the one or the other.
Buschek et al. (2021)	Case study and user test on a working prototype.	Sketch plugin that matches paper-based GUI elements and produces a digital version and creates the wireframes using ML.	AI does not consider design conventions and best practices (e.g., aligning elements, placing them exactly on the same coordinates as in the hand drawing). The authors indicate that it is important to evaluate the output design for such instances and they recommend using ML as the glue between the different design steps, not for replacing designers but rather allowing them to spend more time on creative work.

Feldman (2017a)	Experimental procedure using qualitative techniques and designer feedback.	Evolver, a Creative Artificial Intelligence System (CAIS) that is based on genetic algorithms and designer-controlled constraints.	AI helps designers to augment their creativity and to create something that neither the designer nor AI could do alone. CAISs are efficient and effective, but do not understand the entire problem, and they lack human skills like empathy and emotion. Based on their findings, the authors suggest that the designer cannot be replaced but they will need to use new tools to evolve the design process.
Gomes & Preto (2018)	Conceptual article and artifact design	Focuses on interactions that are boosted by AI and specifically emphasized on the importance of a design oriented approach	A design oriented approach for emotional user experience depends on the interactions that the artefact encourages which are offered to the user per physical and digital interfaces.
Todi et al. (2016)	Two empirical studies involving 20 end users and 10 designers.	Tool for integrating realtime optimization in the design tool. A designer sketches first the layout and receives AI-enabled suggestions to explore design alternatives.	The AI-enabled tool delivers solution similar to what the designers would develop on their own, reducing the overall time necessary, and findings suggest that exploring alternatives like this can be positive.
O'Donovan et al. (2015)	AB testing: comparison of a baseline design to an automatically adapted one. The empirical entailed 20 designers developing 200 design and then 2 designers evaluating the final output.	Design Scape allows for interactive layout suggestions or automatically adapting the design, using a form of ML.	Users overall disliked the adaptive feature because they felt that they were losing control over the design and they preferred being able to ignore optimisation suggestions. Looking at the final output, 63,4% preferred the adaptive design over the baseline, with only 34,1% not having used any suggestions.

Pandian and Suleri (2020)	Conceptual - the paper proposes different solutions for using AI to automate UI design.	MetaMorph: a UI element detector that uses deep neural networks. Blu: a UI layout generator taking screenshots as input and creating blueprints and editable graphics.	As the design process consists of many steps, a designer should not use AI for automating and collapsing all steps into one. MetaMorph and Blu automate parts of the process and allow for customization.
Pandian et al. (2020)	Qualitative study with 10 UX designers undertaking tasks based on prespecified tasks, completing an After-Scenario Questionnaire (ASQ) and participating in interviews.	MetaMorph is used in combination with Eve (Suleri et al. 2019) to help the transition from low-fidelity to high- fidelity prototypes.	MetaMorph detects elements from low-fidelity sketches with mAP of 63,5%, and above averaged answers to all ASQ questions. These results suggest that the process was quick and easy with enough information for completing each task. Part of the recommendations entail allowing designers to correct the detected elements when the later are wrong, to manually detect undetected elements, and include only those elements with high accuracy.
Silva- Rodriguez, Nava-Munoz et al. (2020)	Experimental evaluation of interaction design patterns recommendation mode.	Model for recommending design patterns based on design-level requirements, using supervised ML (logistic regression, multinomial Naive Bayes, linear support vector machine (SVM), and random forest) to help designers choose patterns.	Design patterns increase usability and UX, but selecting the right patterns can be a hard task, especially for inexperienced designers. The implementation of the pattern can reduce the time spent finding the correct patterns. While the study used a small dataset, the findings suggest that ML can be useful for solving this problem.
Zhou et al. (2020)	Design experiment with 11 students and evaluation by 3 experts.	Deep learning solution and field intelligence for helping designers during the iterations of the initial design input.	AI could improve designers' performance in fluency and stylisation, but flexibility and originality did not improve.

Gardey et al. (2022)	Evaluation experiment where 3 UX experts evaluated interaction with widgets across 6 websites.	The authors used decision trees (a type of ML technique) to predict the effort involved in interacting with the widgets.	AI tools and techniques can be used to accurately capture and assess the effort involved in interacting with digital solutions, thus supporting UX evaluation.

AI uses for design evaluation

Once a prototype is finished, it needs to be checked to see if it meets the wants of the users. In this step, user tests or looking at user data are often part of the process. Table 4 is a summary of the research that has already been done on how AI can be used to automate or carry out this step in the planning process.

Most of the research looks at UX using something like a SUS-schema, but there is only one study that looks at using AI to automate the process. With more information, Yang et al. (2020), who study mobile apps, say that UX is evaluated by user data, which can then be used to help creators decide if the design process needs to be repeated. However, the results show that this method can be used to simulate UX to some degree, which makes it faster and easier to find the best design. However, it cannot improve learning or usefulness. This makes it seem like deep learning might not be a good idea during the review process. In fact, one important part of evaluating a design is involving the end user directly, such as through user testing and walkthroughs. This involves qualitative methods to see if user needs have been met, which results in qualitative data. We couldn't find a study that used this kind of approach for evaluating AI-based systems, but some do use more detailed methods along with user testing to look at feedback from users and find patterns using AI. Artificial intelligence (AI) is used in some studies to see how a user might respond to a design. Some scholars say this method could be good enough to replace traditional user testing because it saves time, money, and other resources. Wallach et al. (2020), on the other hand, say that this shouldn't be the end goal because usability testing is the only way to find problems and evaluate user experience. Some people think that the best results will come from a mix of AI and human design. This is because predictive models can give useful information that goes beyond user testing.

Table 4. Uses of AI for designing evaluation

Source	**Research Method**	**Type of AI and solution**	**Key findings**
Swearngin and Li (2019)	Informal evaluation of a solution on the basis of testing for accuracy by 7 interaction designers.	TapShie: a tool that uses deep learning to model how 'tappable' an element is according to a human user.	Automated techniques to cut costs of user studies. Reasonable accuracy in matching how likely a human will think UI element is tappable. The interaction designers saw potential in this solution but expect more functions (e.g., 'tappability' of different screens).
Wallach et al. (2020)	Multiple case studies, using AI for prototyping UI models and evaluated using synthetic designers (machine generated)	ACT-R for ANTETYPE: an extension to the prototyping tool that simulates human behaviour based on cognitive architecture and acting as the designer's "best friend". The designers asks the ML for help and receives performance predictions for a given scenario.	The weakness of AI is linked to low trust, loss of manual skills and lack of situation awareness. This solution supports designers by providing a quick performance analysis of different design variables. The goal is not to replace user testing (which gives rich qualitative insights) but to use AI for gathering quantitative data as well, thus making for a mutually beneficial relationship between UX and AI.
Yang et al. (2020)	The study follows the Artificial Intelligence-Aided Design framework, doing user testing of the old and the new application with 6 participants.	AI application using click behaviour for assessing UX.	The solution is able to simulate UX to a certain extent, resulting in improved efficiency of optimal design, but it is unable to improve learning and effectiveness. It can be used to assist designers, but it is not an omnipotent tool.

Zhou et al. (2020)	Empirical study with 500 participants labelling their preferred solution, the later then used for updating the final model. 20 people later evaluated real- life examples from the Baidu mobile app.	FEELER: an ML approach to explore and evaluate design solutions. It uses collective learning for predictive modelling based on user feedback and measuring preference scores to help designers quickly and conveniently adjust UI modules.	The findings indicate that the solution can help designers to identify the best design solutions, to improve UX, to understand the hidden rules for good design and to test out more options for UIs.

AI uses in the development process

The developer will have to code the user interface after the designer has come up with a solution. Often, there are big differences between the prototype (the UI that the designer designed) and the real UI code (the UI that the developer built). These differences are usually fixed by the developer so that the written UI can still meet the needs of the users that were outlined in the prototype. So, these differences can be given to AI programs by automating the process and turning the prototype into code while still letting the creator be more involved in the development process. We've put together a list of studies that suggest using AI in the making process in Table 5.

Table 5. Uses of AI for development

Source	Research Method	Type of AI and solution	Key findings
Nguyen and Csallner (2015)	Empirical evaluation of 488 screenshots from 100 popular apps.	REMAUI: a tool that identifies interface elements using computer vision and character recognition. It is used for generating user interfaces that are similar to the initial screenshot.	First technique to automatically reverse engineer a mobile application user interface with an average run time of 9 secs.

Beltramelli (2018)	Accuracy testing of a proposed solution.	Converting high-fidelity prototype (screenshots) to code by using deep learning to reverse engineer user interfaces from a single input image.	The solution was trained on a small data sets and supports few parameters, but proved to be able to learn the layout and achieved 77% of validation accuracy. There were problems with colour selection, the correct GUI style and modelling GUIs with long lists.
Chen et al. (2018)	Accuracy testing and generalisation and usefulness evaluation of a proposed solution. UI-exploration effectiveness is measured using the Monkey tool (developed by Google) and user stories were piloted with 8 PhD students.	Stoat: a system that transforms UI design image to a GUI skeleton using computer vision and machine translation. It creates an automated GUI exploration framework for building datasets for training purposes.	Large datasets were used and tested and the solution achieved high speed, reliability, accuracy and generalisation. During pilot testing, it achieved 90% satisfaction and the results indicate that this solution saves time when used as a baseline, and being updated based on results.
Asiroglu et al. (2019)	Accuracy testing of a proposed solution.	The solution automates code generation of low- fidelity prototype (hand drawn mock-ups) via object detection, object cropping, object recognition, and HTML building. It uses computer vision and deep learning using CNN.	The solution achieved 96% method accuracy and 73% validation accuracy.
Fernandez-Garcia et al. (2019)	Case Study	Recommender systems using neural networks that help end users choose what is displayed and adapting in real time.	The solution simplifies the process when there is a large number of components to choose from. Neural network model achieves 80% performance accuracy.

Latipova et al. (2019)	Review of child computer interaction educational projects.	The focus was on examining FloydHub, Pix2Code and Sketch-2Code to identify how neural networks can be used for child computer interaction educational projects by automatically creating GUIs.	Automatically generating code can make it easier to include children in the design process, because they are able to interact with their ideas faster, with lower costs and greater ease of use. Challenges of neural networks include accuracy, and needing suitable data sets.
Souza Baule et al. (2020)	Literature review of 20 approaches for using code automation for GUI design.	Mapping of studies that automate code based on GUI design im- ages using deep learning and computer vision.	The review shows that ML can facilitate and speed up the design process, whereby designers will still be able to remain creative during the initial steps of the design process. Different approaches are used for automating code (from classic ML to CNNs), and the review identifies some common weaknesses.
Moran et al. (2020)	Empirical study on accuracy testing via interviews with industrial practitioners.	ReDraw: a system that automates the move from GUI to code via detection, classification, and assembly using computer vision and neural networks.	The solution achieves average component classification accuracy of 91%. It accurately detects components, and creates a visually similar solution with reasonable code structure with reasonable hierarchies. Only two mock-up artifacts were examined.
Dave et al. (2021)	Review of 3 ML- based approaches.	The study compares different ML methods (low-fidelity HTML Code Generation, sketch2code and pix-2code) for converting UIs to code.	All three methods aims to reduce the effort and time so as to facilitate rapid prototyping and good results. The different approaches apply to different levels of prototype, and therefore each has different drawbacks and benefits.

As was already said, the main goal of development is to turn a concept into code. In fact, our research shows that most of the studies are focused on the growth step. All of the studies use machine learning to turn samples into code, and most of them use computer vision to find parts. So, computer vision seems very useful since its ability to find objects can be used to find GUIs and write code.

We found a lot of different kinds of machine learning being used, from simpler ones like CNN to more complicated ones like more traditional ones. ML seems to be used in the design process in line with the trend of using these kinds of algorithms to automate boring and time-consuming tasks. ML is used a lot, which shows it has a lot of potential in the field. This is especially true since all of the methods that were tested were able to find design elements and turn a prototype into code. Most of them were also able to make code that kept the hierarchical structure of the graphic elements. So, Moran et al. (2020) use neural networks to go from a graphical user interface (GUI) to real code, and Asiroglou et al. (2019) use deep learning and CNN to go from low to high accuracy.

But there are some problems with all of these ideas for using AI. For example, many of these methods can only find a few of the parts that make something up. In many cases, the researchers also didn't test their answer with real end users and designers, or they only tested it in small ways. Instead, they tested and measured how accurate the ML system was, which can lead to results that aren't true. These are some other common weaknesses:

- The merging of design elements when these are close together - the same applies for texts positioned close together when they use similar fonts;
- Incorrect classification of smaller design elements;
- Incorrect implementation of the alternative GUI elements;
- Incorrect classification/misclassification of progress bars and toggle buttons when the design uses multiple styles;
- Low accuracy and simplistic GUI skeletons; and
- Non recognisable GUI elements when they are not fully visible.

Because of this weakness, some authors say that automatic code generation should only be used as an addition to design and development to save time before the authors work on improving and updating their design and finishing their own development.

As was already said, most studies look at how to use ML to automatically code a prototype while it is being made. Fernandez-Garcia et al. (2019), on the other hand, suggest using a suggestion model to help end users pick what is shown to them. This shows another way AI could be used during development: to allow users to customize what they see.

The Shift in Digital Design Processes Due to AI

Once we read the chosen articles, we see that they all have some important things in common when it comes to how AI might affect and change the digital design process. AI is an area with many sub-technologies, so it's interesting to see that all of the studies that have been found use some kind of ML algorithm. One possible reason for this is that designers and developers can get a lot out of using weak AI that is driven by machine learning. These benefits come from weak AI being easier to build and use than strong AI, which means it needs fewer resources and is easier to put into action. So, weak AI is a good place for makers to start, especially if they don't have a lot of experience in this area. AI, on the other hand, is growing at a speed that has never been seen before, and the subtechnologies that support it offer a wide range of uses and a complete set of tools. It shows that neural networks, deep learning, and DNNs are getting a lot of attention. These technologies, along with computer vision, can be used in the planning process. When new and complicated technologies are used, designers and end users may not fully understand how these technologies can affect not only the design process but also the final product, which is the digital solution. This isn't always a problem with skills or a lack of them. Instead, it's because AI is a "black box" technology that can't explain how decisions are made. Because of this, even if AI-enabled digital solutions work, designers and end users won't be able to easily figure out the causal relationships that support them. This is a big problem because the design process today depends on close collaboration between designers and end users.

Another issue that the studies look at is the part of the designer in a design process that uses AI. However, the studies give different points of view. Some people say that AI can be a good designer on its own, potentially taking the place of human designers. Others are more positive and say that human designers and AI should work together to make things better for everyone. Kaiser (2019), for example, says that AI can automate the design process by using large datasets to build strong models that can mimic the steps that human designers take. However, it is unlikely that this will completely get rid of the need for human designers in the design process. However, very few studies have looked at the first two steps in the design process—understanding and describing the context of use and describing user requirements. These steps require interaction between the design and end users and use a lot of resources (i.e., are easy to automate). Because of this, it's more possible that AI and UX designers will need to work together, with AI helping humans make AI-enabled solutions (2019). These kinds of partnerships between humans and AI will be key to properly incorporating AI into the design process. This is because AI can't directly understand and use the unspoken information that goes into making digital projects. To work together, though, UX designers will need to learn more about AI and machine learning (ML) so they know what kinds of problems AI can and can't fix.

We also think that AI will be used more to make the more boring parts of the planning process automatic. For this reason, low-fidelity samples are simple to feed into the AI tool, which can then make the executable code more quickly. This can save a lot of resources, especially if changes need to be made to the sample. They can get back their time by automating jobs they do over and over again. This way, they can focus on improving their creativity, skills, and abilities, paying more attention to their end users, and figuring out what problems they need to solve and how to do it. But there are two parts to the design process: setting the problem and solving it. Solving the problem includes coming up with ideas, making prototypes, iterating, and then critically analyzing the solution. This could lead to constant changes until the best solution is found. However, not all of these tasks can or should be automated. Because of this, the whole design process shouldn't be thought of as a single AI-enabled process. Instead, it's important to tell the difference between "getting the right thing" (finding the problem that needs to be solved) and "getting the thing right" (finding the best answer in terms of features and ease of use).

Planning for the Future

There are many parts of the UX design process that could be changed drastically by AI. However, recent progress, especially in the area of creative AI, has opened up a whole new set of possibilities. The newest wave of generative AI is expected to completely change how digital solution creators plan, build, and test their apps. Early uses of generative AI have shown that these tools can produce writing, code, images, and other types of media that are just as good as those made by professionals with a lot of experience. There are actually more and more articles that talk about how to use tools like ChatGPT to make code for different kinds of apps, which speeds up the process of releasing new digital designs. As of the time this review was written, there weren't many research papers talking about how generative AI is used in the UX design process. Still, reading current news stories and practitioner reports shows that there are a lot of very interesting uses and applications that could be made.

Opening up generative AI tools to more people is becoming more popular because they let more people do things that need a lot of specialized knowledge, like coding and design. This means that answers that used to be only available to highly skilled professionals are now easier for regular people to get. Something similar happened in the early days of the internet, when building and designing websites was something that only a few very skilled people could do. This doesn't mean that creative AI tools will replace the UX design process. Instead, it means that these tools will make design more open to more people. It has also been shown that creative AI tools are very good at gathering and analyzing different kinds of data and coming up with new ideas. These kinds of programs can help a lot with figuring out what users want and turning that into useful design elements. As well as that, generative AI apps can act as testers or even help find problems with design or usefulness by taking on different roles. For example, generative AI can help find or even make different design options that meet user needs when it comes to universal design. It can also make suggestions that human designers might not have thought of. In the coming years, we may see different types of UX designers working together with generative AI. Also, many design jobs will likely be automated and transferred through generative AI services, making it easier for people who aren't very good at design to make digital things.

Research Agenda

Table 6. A Research Agenda for the use of AI in the digital design process

Theme	Open issue	Research Question
Theme 1: Automating the design process with AI	• Limited knowledge of which parts of design should be automated • Unclear understanding of how the nature of work for designers' changes when automating parts of the design process • Lack of knowledge about strengths and weaknesses of AI vs humans in certain design process steps • Limited understanding of how to streamline data integration throughout the design process when using AI tools	• What design process stages are more suitable for automation? • How does the nature of work change for designers with the introduction of AI? • What are the informational flows in the design process and how can designers improve them to develop optimal solutions?

Theme 2: (Co) Creating with AI	• Unclear understanding what will be the required skills and competences for those involved in an AI-enabled user centred design process. • Limited understanding of how end users should or could participate in the design process.	• What will be the required skills and competencies of UX and UI designers and developers, and how will these evolve over time? • What are the possible changes required for the integration of AI-enabled user centred design approaches at business/organisational level? • What are the potential opportunities for including more diverse end users in the design process?
Theme 3: Negative effects of AI use in digital design	• Lack of knowledge regarding responsibility of projects with the introduction of AI • Limited understanding of how AI use in the design process influences project outcomes • Lack of understanding of how AI use in the design process may influence designer involvement • Lack of explainability can create problems in collaboration between designers and customers	• What are the negative effects of the introduction of AI on designer work performance? • What potential threats around data privacy does AI use introduce? • How does the mechanization of parts of the design process with AI influence customer-designer's relationships? • How can explainability be incorporated in AI tools for the design process?

We found three main ideas about how AI might change the digital design process in the future by putting together what was already written in Section 4. These are put together into a study agenda in this section. It builds on open questions and key assumptions and is meant to be a starting point for future research and practice. Each of the three study themes is meant to show where there are gaps in the current body of research and suggest ways to fill them so that AI can help the design process in a useful way. First, we talk about why these research themes are important for the conversation about AI use in digital design. Next, we present a number of research questions within each theme that can lead to more study.

In Table 6, you can see a summary of the themes and some open study questions that go along with them.

Figure 4. Synthesized existing knowledge on AI use for UX design process and future research directions

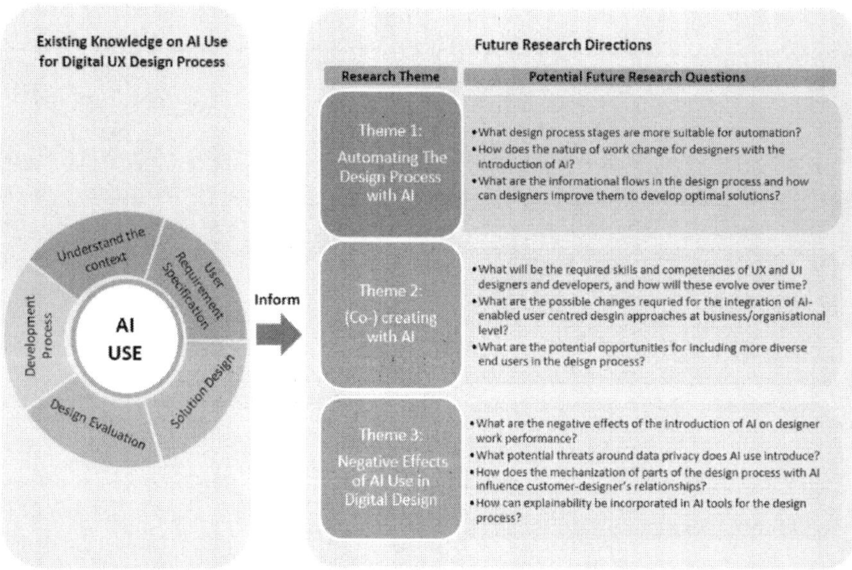

Theme 1: Automating the design process with AI

At this point, machine learning is mostly used in digital design because it's easy to get data, with little attention paid to user-centered design. More study needs to be done on how to systematically use AI to define design patterns, teach designers, and make prototypes of tools. At the moment, this kind of automation in key steps of the design process isn't getting enough attention, even though it's very useful. According to Buschek et al. (2021), it is important not to use AI just because it is possible to do so. In particular, some people say that AI technologies should only be used to automate tasks that are very time-consuming and need a lot of human work. This is especially true when AI is used for artistic design work. It's important to figure out what problems designers face and what boring, repetitive tasks they have to do, as well as how AI can be used to handle these tasks and help designers come up with new ideas. For this to work, we need to know a lot about the specific tasks and daily work that designers do in different situations. We also need to put AI apps that automate important tasks at the top of the list. In addition, it shows how important it is to use AI to come up with ideas or patterns that can help artists' work by making them more creative.

Because there are many steps and activities in the design process, it is also important to know how automating some parts might change the jobs that the designer has to do and the process as a whole. As was already shown, when AI is used, creators need to give it information about what results they want from digital design. In this way, designers don't just focus on layout; they also learn how to formalize the mental, structural, functional, and aesthetic parts of design. This process needs people to be creative, solve problems, make sense of things, have understanding, and work together. For AI technologies to be used more in the design process, it is important to understand how parts of these tasks can be given to AI systems and how that changes the kind of work designers do.

In a new paper from 2021, Buschek et al. argue about what tasks AI technologies should not or should not be able to do automatically. The reasoning behind their case is that humans or AI technologies may be better at some parts of the design process, so it wouldn't make sense to change how the work is set up. But there are also many times when AI technologies can be used in places where non-digital answers have been used in the past. For instance, because digital mockups can be made faster than paper mock-ups, testing and gathering usage data can begin earlier. It is very important to know how this change in the process affects the end design and how well it works. Keeping track of how the use of AI to automate certain parts of the design process changes depending on the industry or other internal factors can also help us learn more about the possible problems that could arise when these tools are put to use. Future study should try to figure out how to make tools that take away the boring parts of designing and testing while making the creative parts better.

There are also not many studies that look at the whole planning process from the research that has been done so far. Because of this, many tools have been made that make the work of creating easier. So, one area of study that could be done in the future is how the fragmentation of the design process and the tools that come after it affect the results. More study can be done to find out if using more than one AI tool leads to better results or if using solutions that work together leads to better data flow and better results. Some papers, like Moran et al.'s (2020), say that more research should be done to make the whole process possible. Dave et al. (2021) backs this up by saying, "there is a huge amount of room for improvement, and as machine learning algorithms get better, the possibilities of intelligent automation, especially in the area of website creation, will greatly expand."

Theme 2: (Co)creating with AI

Adding AI to the design process will obviously change the design process and the way things get done. These changes will have to do with who can and should be involved in the planning process. There are changes that will happen because AI is automating the design process, and there are changes that will happen because designers will need to learn new skills.

At this point, the design process includes UX and UI designers and developers. They are in charge of coming up with ideas for a product or service, designing it, and then building it. This is especially true for user-centered design. At the same time, this process often involves many people, such as the client who ordered the product or service and, more and more, the people who will use it in the future. In particular, the user-centered design process has changed over the years from seeing the "user as subject" to seeing the "user as partner." This means that future end users are involved in all stages of design and development, and they help make the final product along with designers and developers.

But there are a lot of problems and restrictions that come up during these kinds of co-creation processes. When this comes to designers in particular, they often have to do more than just design. They have to act as researchers too, watching how people behave, encouraging their creativity, and making it easier for them to use the different AI tools that are used for design. But designers and developers might not have the skills and knowledge to support these kinds of approaches that involve a lot of people. You also need hard skills to use AI tools in the planning process. This means that you need to know how to use and manipulate these tools. One example is Yang et al. (2020), who talk about how UX designers, for example, don't know enough about DNNs. Because of this, it is very important to know what skills and knowledge UX and UI designers and developers will need in the near and far future so that they can keep up with the fast pace of AI progress. At the same time, as companies and businesses switch from innovation systems that rely on humans to systems that rely on AI, they will likely need to make more changes on the inside. These changes will mostly need to be made to the business processes that interact with design processes, which use AI tools and techniques. In Industry 4.0, Ngoc et al. (2022) found that the value chain of a business needs to be changed so that people and AI can work together in a formal and useful way. This is especially true when it comes to human-centered design and the growing use of AI. Because of this, future study could look into the kinds of changes that need to be made and how those changes will affect businesses and organizations.

However, the use of AI in the design process has opened up important new possibilities. According to Latipova et al. (2019), AI can make the planning process easier for more people, like children and people with disabilities, to be a part of. This is because AI makes things more accessible, which makes them more inclusive. In fact, user-centered design takes time and money, which limits how creators interact with a wide range of users. One way to fix this problem is to use simulators, which can simulate different impairments and tell creators what users can and can't do. AI, on the other hand, can help make more customized solutions, which is good for both the designer and the end user. For example, AI can help the designer by suggesting activities, and it can also help the end user by making interactions more useful and easier for defining requirements. However, since research in this area is still in its early stages, it will be important to find out more about how AI can help and guide new efforts to do inclusive user research, while also taking into account any unexpected effects that might happen as a result.

Theme 3: Negative effects of AI use in digital design

By learning about the problems or issues that might come up when using AI tools in the planning process, we can better figure out how to include and improve these tools. One good way to look into this problem would be to have designers take part in the study and learn about the limits that AI puts on their work. Also, the way their jobs are changing could have bad effects, like making them more stressed out because they have to use new technologies or making it harder for them to use these tools in real life. It's also possible that automating some parts of the design process could hurt the quality of the final goods or make designers feel less responsible for the digital solutions they create. Because of this, it is important to know what the bad effects could be of using AI in digital creation so that the right methods can be found for using them.

Up to now, studies that looked at the performance of digital goods were the only ones that looked at the possible bad effects of using AI in digital design. Digital goods might meet customer needs, but the way they are implemented could be very different from what was planned. This is why it's important to know how the use of AI affects the relationship between the customer and the creator throughout the whole development process. For example, AI applications that are based on data may require customers to give designers large amounts of quantitative data or possibly private information. Also, the high cost of brand-new AI apps could make it more expensive to offer digital design solutions to customers, which could hurt the success of the project. Because of this, we need to understand how AI is used in a wider sense, not just in the planning process but in the whole relationship between a customer and a service provider.

Lastly, Buschek et al. (2021) show a possible bad result of using AI in the design process: they say that using these tools may turn designers into people who just use tools that produce results on their own. Because of this, designers might go with what AI tools suggest even if they don't fully understand how they came up with certain ideas or design principles. When you think about how many people are usually involved in a design job, this problem gets even worse. This means that jobs that are done automatically by AI need to be more reliable and consistent, and they also need to use common definitions for information. An important part of making the process and acceptance clear is making sure that everyone understands and follows the same rules for how these systems work. Adding explainability to insights or suggested solutions also helps designers know why and how AI tools suggest certain solutions. It also lowers the risk of blindly using AI ideas because it gives designers more time to think about them. Therefore, one interesting area of study is to find out how adding explainability to AI algorithms can help designers do their jobs better.

Discussion and Conclusion

Digital solution users today expect professional and easy-to-use experiences. This means that designers and developers have to keep improving their work and delivering high-quality goods. Iterative design processes that balance originality with general design principles are often needed to come up with solutions that meet these standards. Professionals in the field have thought about how AI can be used to help with this. We've put together what we already know about how AI might be used in the future, which will change how digital solutions are designed.

We used a method called "systematic literature review" to find and write down relevant evidence from previous research. We then used the User Centered Design Framework to organize and present our results in a way that showed the main steps of the design process. Our goal was to present our results in a way that would draw attention to the most important suggested uses and applications of AI for creating digital solutions, while also keeping track of the specific AI tools and techniques that were suggested. The main focus has been on showing the current state of the art in AI use as well as how designers think AI could be used in the future.

As far as theoretical applications go, our results give researchers a clear picture of the steps involved in UX design and development, along with ways that AI can be used in some or all of them. In particular, we broke down our results into seven separate parts. The first five parts are based on the five steps of the user-centered design process, and the last two parts show how AI can be used in more than one step and throughout the whole design process. This method better shows the wide range of AI uses and new opportunities because we think that looking at things from the designer's point of view and studying the main tasks that go into UX design and development gives us a fuller picture of how AI is being used now, as well as the main problems and changes it is causing for different groups. It also lets researchers use ideas and methods from other fields that can help them study AI for UX design by putting them in the right context.

Through our research agenda, we also find a number of areas that need more study so that we can learn more about how AI can be used and when it should and shouldn't be used in the UX design process. The suggested research plan is not a complete list of topics that researchers should look into. However, it does point researchers in the direction of some of the most important topics that will be popular in the next few years.

From a practical point of view, this part tells practitioners what we know about how AI can be used for UX design right now. This body of knowledge can help designers and developers come up with new goods or services or figure out what areas are very important. For instance, our results show that some parts of UX design can be automated in certain situations. They also show the tools and methods that can be used when they are needed. Some of these technologies are already in use, like when designing websites. We think that these kinds of tools could also be used in software engineering and interface design, but it would depend on the situation.

This chapter has tried to give you a broad look at the field of AI use in the UX design process, but it does have some flaws. Our first step in the UX design process was to look at the user-centered design method. There are many people who use this process, especially in academia, but workers also use other processes. So, in the future, researchers can look into different ways that UX designers do their work, or they could even create whole new methods that use AI. Also, our chapter was limited by the written work that was available. As the field of AI moves quickly forward, especially with the rise of generative AI, it's likely that academic papers still don't cover the newest developments in UX and AI use. So, one interesting area of study that could be done would be to get first-hand information from professionals who use these kinds of tools in their daily work. This way of doing study might lead to the discovery of new ways to use AI to help with UX design.

Finally, we want to stress that our results and plans are based on a thorough analysis of past research, which does have some issues. The first step in most methods for systematic literature reviews is to use keywords to create search strings and run queries through databases. Usually, these queries only go as deep as the chapter title and abstract. This means that studies that don't use the set keywords in the title or abstract will almost certainly be missed and not included in the final group of papers. In this chapter, we tried to solve this problem by doing both forward and backward searches, which helped us find and analyze more articles that didn't use the predefined keywords but instead used different words. A bigger problem is that systematic literature reviews always look back at the past because they only look at information that was available up to a certain point in time. It's possible that important articles published after this set date will completely change how we think about AI for UX design. This is because AI is developing so quickly.

References

Abbas, A. M. H., Ghauth, K. I., & Ting, C.-Y. (2022). User Experience Design Using Machine Learning: A Systematic Review. IEEE Access, 10, 51501-51514. https://doi.org/10.1109/ACCESS.2022.3173289

Agner, L., Necyk, B., & Renzi, A. (2020). Recommendation Systems and Machine Learning: Mapping the User Experience. In A. Marcus & E. Rosenzweig (Eds.), Design, User Experience, and Usability. Design for Contemporary Interactive Environments (pp. 3-17). Springer International Publishing. https://doi.org/10.1007/978-3-030-49760-6_1

Asatiani, A., Malo, P., Nagbol, P. R., Penttinen, E., Rinta-Kahila, T., & Salovaara, A. (2020). Challenges of Explaining the Behavior of Black-Box AI Systems. MIS Quarterly Executive, 19(4), 259-278.

Asiroglu, B., Mete, B. R., Yildiz, E., Nalcakan, Y., Sezen, A., Dagtekin, M., & Ensari, T. (2019). Automatic HTML Code Generation from Mock-Up Images Using Machine Learning Techniques. 2019 Scientific Meeting on Electrical-Electronics & Biomedical Engineering and Computer Science (EBBT), 1-4. https://doi.org/10.1109/EBBT.2019.8741736

Beltramelli, T. (2018). pix2code: Generating Code from a Graphical User Interface Screenshot. Proceedings of the ACM SIGCHI Symposium on Engineering Interactive Computing Systems, 1-6. https://doi.org/10.1145/3220134.3220135

Buschek, D., Anlauff, C., & Lachner, F. (2021). Paper2Wire - A Case Study of User-Centred Development of Machine Learning Tools for UX Designers. I-Com, 20(1), 19-32. https://doi.org/10.1515/icom-2021- 0002

Cardoso, C., & Clarkson, P. J. (2012). Simulation in user-centred design: Helping designers to empathise with atypical users. Journal of Engineering Design, 23(1), 1-22. https://doi.org/10.1080/09544821003742650

Chatterjee, S., & Kar, A. K. (2017). Effects of successful adoption of information technology enabled services in proposed smart cities of India: From user experience perspective. Journal of Science and Technology Policy Management, 9(2), 189-209. https://doi.org/10.1108/JSTPM-03-2017-0008

Chaudhuri, N. B., Dhar, D., & Yammiyavar, P. G. (2022a). A computational model for subjective evaluation of novelty in descriptive aptitude. International Journal of Technology and Design Education, 32(2), 11211158. https://doi.org/10.1007/s10798-020-09638-2

Chaudhuri, N. B., Dhar, D., & Yammiyavar, P. G. (2022b). Automating assessment of design exams: A case study of novelty evaluation. Expert Systems with Applications, 189, 116108. https://doi.org/10.1016/j.eswa.2021.116108

Chen, C., Su, T., Meng, G., Xing, Z., & Liu, Y. (2018). From UI design image to GUI skeleton: A neural machine translator to bootstrap mobile GUI implementation. Proceedings of the 40th International Conference on Software Engineering, 665-676. https://doi.org/10.1145/3180155.3180240

Christoforakos, L., & Diefenbach, S. (2019). Idealization Effects in UX Evaluation at Early Concept Stages: Challenges of Low-Fidelity Prototyping. In T. Z. Ahram & C. Falcao (Eds.), Advances in Usability, User Experience and Assistive Technology (pp. 3-14). Springer International Publishing. https://doi.org/10.1007/978-3-319-94947-5_1

Dave, H., Sonje, S., Pardeshi, J., Chaudhari, S., & Raundale, P. (2021). A survey on Artificial Intelligence based techniques to convert User Interface design mock-ups to code. 2021 International Conference on Artificial Intelligence and Smart Systems (ICAIS), 28-33. https://doi.org/10.1109/ICAIS50930.2021.9395994

Desolda, G., Esposito, A., Lanzilotti, R., & Costabile, M. F. (2020). Interplay between AI and HCI for UX evaluation: The SERENE case study.

Duan, P., Wierzynski, C., & Nachman, L. (2020). Optimizing User Interface Layouts via Gradient Descent. Proceedings of the 2020 CHI Conference on Human Factors in Computing Systems, 1 -12. https://doi.org/10.1145/3313831.3376589

Enholm, I. M., Papagiannidis, E., Mikalef, P., & Krogstie, J. (2021). Artificial Intelligence and Business Value: A Literature Review. Information Systems Frontiers. https://doi.org/10.1007/s10796-021-10186-w

Feldman, S. (Salevati). (2017a). Co-Creation: Human and AI Collaboration in Creative Expression. Proceedings of the Conference on Electronic Visualisation and the Arts, 422-429. https://doi.org/10.14236/ewic/EVA2017.84

Feldman, S. (Salevati). (2017b, July 1). Co-Creation: Human and AI Collaboration in Creative Expression. Electronic Visualisation and the Arts (EVA 2017) (EVA). https://doi.org/10.14236/ewic/EVA2017.84

Fernandez-Garcia, A. J., Iribarne, L., Corral, A., Criado, J., & Wang, J. Z. (2019). A recommender system for component-based applications using machine learning techniques. Knowledge-Based Systems, 164, 68 84. https://doi.org/10.1016/j.knosys.2018.10.019

Gaffney, G. (2017). The Revolution Will Not Be Handheld. Journal of Usability Studies, 12(3), 92-94.
Gardey, J. C., Grigera, J., Rodriguez, A., Rossi, G., & Garrido, A. (2022). Predicting interaction effort in web interface widgets. International Journal of Human-Computer Studies,168, 102919. https://doi.org/10.1016/jjjhcs.2022.102919

Gomes, C. C., & Preto, S. (2018). Artificial Intelligence and Interaction Design for a Positive Emotional User Experience. In W. Karwowski & T. Ahram (Eds.), Intelligent Human Systems Integration (pp. 62-68). Springer International Publishing. https://doi.org/10.1007/978-3-319-73888-8_11

Gozalo-Brizuela, R., & Garrido-Merchan, E. C. (2023). ChatGPT is not all you need. A State of the Art Review of large Generative AI models. arXiv preprint arXiv:2301.04655.

Hart, J., & Sutcliffe, A. (2019). Is it all about the Apps or the Device?: User experience and technology acceptance among iPad users. International Journal of Human-Computer Studies, 130, 93-112. https://doi.org/10.1016/j.ijhcs.2019.05.002

ISO 9241-210:2010. (2010). ISO 9241-210:2010(en), Ergonomics of human-system interaction—Part 210: Human-centred design for interactive systems. https://www.iso.org/obp/ui/#iso:std:iso:9241:-210:ed- 1:v1:en

Johnston, V., Black, M., Wallace, J., Mulvenna, M., & Bond, R. (2019). A Framework for the Development of a Dynamic Adaptive Intelligent User Interface to Enhance the User Experience. Proceedings of the 31st European Conference on Cognitive Ergonomics, 32-35. https://doi.org/10.1145/3335082.3335125

Kaiser, Z. (2019). Creativity as Computation: Teaching Design in the Age of Automation. Design and Culture, 11(2), 173-192. https://doi.org/10.1080/17547075.2019.1609279

Karimi, P., Grace, K., Maher, M. L., & Davis, N. (2018). Evaluating Creativity in Computational Co-Creative Systems (arXiv:1807.09886). arXiv. https://doi.org/10.48550/arXiv.1807.09886

Koch, J. (2017). Design implications for Designing with a Collaborative AI (Technical Report SS-17-04; The AAAI 2017 Spring Symposium on Designing the User Experience of Machine Learning Systems, p. 4). Association for the Advancement of Artificial Intelligence. https://www.aaai.org/ocs/index.php/SSS/SSS17/paper/viewFile/15382/14577

Korhonen, H., Arrasvuori, J., & Vaananen-Vainio-Mattila, K. (2010). Analysing user experience of personal mobile products through contextual factors. Proceedings of the 9th International Conference on Mobile and Ubiquitous Multimedia, 1-10. https://doi.org/10.1145/1899475.1899486

Latipova, A., Gasenko, A., & Sim, G. (2019). On 'Artificial Intelligence-User Interface' Approach. 2019 International Multi-Conference on Engineering, Computer and Information Sciences (SIBIRCON), 0446-0451. https://doi.org/10.1109/SIBIRCON48586.2019.8958406

Li, S. (2020). The Trend and Characteristic of AI in Art Design. Journal of Physics: Conference Series, 1624(5), 052028. https://doi.Org/10.1088/1742-6596/1624/5/052028

McKenna-Aspell, J., Wang, Y., Rutter, S., & Zamani, E. D. (2022). Facilitating inclusive spaces for sharing untold stories from diverse perspectives. ASIS&T European Chapter IST 2022. Information Science Trends 2022: Untold Stories in Information Science, Sheffield, UK.

Moran, K., Bernal-Cardenas, C., Curcio, M., Bonett, R., & Poshyvanyk, D. (2020). Machine Learning-Based Prototyping of Graphical User Interfaces for Mobile Apps. IEEE Transactions on Software Engineering, 46(2), 196-221. https://doi.org/10.1109/TSE.2018.2844788

Nayernia, H., Bahemia, H., & Papagiannidis, S. (2021). A systematic review of the implementation of industry 4.0 from the organisational perspective. International Journal of Production Research, 1-32. https://doi.org/10.1080/00207543.2021.2002964

Nguyen Ngoc, H., Lasa, G., & Iriarte, I. (2022). Human-centred design in industry 4.0: Case study review and opportunities for future research. Journal of Intelligent Manufacturing, 33(1), 35-76. https://doi.org/10.1007/s10845-021-01796-x

Nguyen, T. A., & Csallner, C. (2015). Reverse Engineering Mobile Application User Interfaces with REMAUI (T). 2015 30th IEEE/ACMInternational Conference on Automated Software Engineering (ASE), 248259. https://doi.org/10.1109/ASE.2015.32

Nilsson, N. J. (1998). Artificial Intelligence: A New Synthesis (1st Edition). Morgan Kaufmann.

Nisafani, A. S., Kiely, G., & Mahony, C. (2020). Workers' technostress: A review of its causes, strains, inhibitors, and impacts. Journal of Decision Systems, 29(sup1), 243-258. https://doi.org/10.1080/12460125.2020.1796286

O'Donovan, P., Agarwala, A., & Hertzmann, A. (2015). DesignScape: Design with Interactive Layout Suggestions. Proceedings of the 33rd Annual ACM Conference on Human Factors in Computing Systems, 1221-1224. https://doi.org/10.1145/2702123.2702149

Oh, C., Song, J., Choi, J., Kim, S., Lee, S., & Suh, B. (2018). I Lead, You Help but Only with Enough Details: Understanding User Experience of Co-Creation with Artificial Intelligence. Proceedings of the 2018 CHI Conference on Human Factors in Computing Systems, 1-13. https://doi.org/10.1145/3173574.3174223

Oulasvirta, A., Dayama, N. R., Shiripour, M., John, M., & Karrenbauer, A. (2020). Combinatorial Optimization of Graphical User Interface Designs. Proceedings of the IEEE, 108(3), 434-464. https://doi.org/10.1109/JPROC.2020.2969687

Pandian, V. P. S., & Suleri, S. (2020). BlackBox Toolkit: Intelligent Assistance to UI Design (arXiv:2004.01949). arXiv. https://doi.org/10.48550/arXiv.2004.01949

Park, J., Han, S. H., Kim, H. K., Cho, Y., & Park, W. (2013). Developing Elements of User Experience for Mobile Phones and Services: Survey, Interview, and Observation Approaches. Human Factors and Ergonomics in Manufacturing & Service Industries, 23(4), 279-293. https://doi.org/10.1002/hfm.20316 Preece, J., Sharp, H., & Rogers, Y. (2015). Interaction Design: Beyond Human-Computer Interaction (4th edition). John Wiley.

Salminen, J., Sengun, S., Jung, S., & Jansen, B. J. (2019). Design Issues in Automatically Generated Persona Profiles: A Qualitative Analysis from 38 Think-Aloud Transcripts. Proceedings of the 2019 Conference on Human Information Interaction and Retrieval, 225-229. https://doi.org/10.1145/3295750.3298942

Sanders, E. B.-N., & Stappers, P. J. (2008). Co-creation and the new landscapes of design. CoDesign, 4(1), 518. https://doi.org/10.1080/15710880701875068

Schmidt, A., & Etches, A. (2014). Useful, Usable, Desirable: Applying User Experience Design to Your Library. ALA Editions.

Sermuga Pandian, V. P., Suleri, S., Beecks, C., & Jarke, M. (2020). MetaMorph: AI Assistance to Transform Lo- Fi Sketches to Higher Fidelities. 32nd Australian Conference on Human-Computer Interaction, 403-412. https://doi.org/10.1145/3441000.3441030

Silva-Rodriguez, V., Nava-Munoz, S. E., Castro, L. A., Martinez-Perez, F. E., Perez-Gonzalez, H. G., & Torres- Reyes, F. (2020). Classifying design-level requirements using machine learning for a recommender of interaction design patterns. IET Software, 14(5), 544-552. https://doi.org/10.1049/iet-sen.2019.0291

Souza Baule, D. de, Wangenheim, C. G. von, Wangenheim, A., & Hauck, J. C. R. (2020). Recent Progress in Automated Code Generation from GUI Images Using Machine Learning Techniques. JUCS - Journal of Universal Computer Science, 26(9), 1095-1127. https://doi.org/10.3897/jucs.2020.058

Suleri, S., Sermuga Pandian, V. P., Shishkovets, S., & Jarke, M. (2019). Eve: A Sketch-based Software Prototyping Workbench. Extended Abstracts of the 2019 CHI Conference on Human Factors in Computing Systems, 1-6. https://doi.org/10.1145/3290607.3312994

Sun, L., Zhou, Z., Wu, W., Zhang, Y., Zhang, R., & Xiang, W. (2020). Developing a Toolkit for Prototyping Machine Learning-Empowered Products: International Journal of Design, 14(2), 16.

Swearngin, A., & Li, Y. (2019). Modeling Mobile Interface Tappability Using Crowdsourcing and Deep Learning. Proceedings of the 2019 CHI Conference on Human Factors in Computing Systems, 1-11. https://doi.org/10.1145/3290605.3300305

Tian, H., Lu, W., Li, T. O., Tang, X., Cheung, S. C., Klein, J., & Bissyande, T. F. (2023). Is ChatGPT the Ultimate Programming Assistant--How far is it?. arXiv preprint arXiv:2304.11938.

Todi, K., Weir, D., & Oulasvirta, A. (2016). Sketchplore: Sketch and Explore with a Layout Optimiser. Proceedings of the 2016 ACM Conference on Designing Interactive Systems, 543-555. https://doi.org/10.1145/2901790.2901817

Tokkonen, H., & Saariluoma, P. (2013). How user experience is understood? 2013 Science and Information Conference, 791-795.

Tranfield, D., Denyer, D., & Smart, P. (2003a). Towards a Methodology for Developing Evidence-Informed Management Knowledge by Means of Systematic Review. British Journal of Management, 14(3), 207-222. https://doi.org/10.1111/1467-8551.00375

Tranfield, D., Denyer, D., & Smart, P. (2003b). Towards a Methodology for Developing Evidence-Informed Management Knowledge by Means of Systematic Review. British Journal of Management, 14(3), 207-222. https://doi.org/10.1111/1467-8551.00375

Verganti, R., Vendraminelli, L., & Iansiti, M. (2020). Innovation and Design in the Age of Artificial Intelligence. Journal of Product Innovation Management, 37(3), 212-227. https://doi.org/10.1111/jpim.12523

Wallach, D., Flohr, L., & Kaltenhauser, A. (2020). Beyond the Buzzwords: On the Perspective of AI in UX and Vice Versa. International Conference on Human-Computer Interaction, 146-166. https://doi.org/10.1007/978-3-030-50334-5_10

Wilson, C. (2013). Interview Techniques for UX Practitioners: A User-Centered Design Method. Newnes.

Yang, B., Wei, L., & Pu, Z. (2020). Measuring and Improving User Experience Through Artificial Intelligence- Aided Design. Frontiers in Psychology, 11, 595374.

Yang, Q. (2017). The Role of Design in Creating Machine-Learning-Enhanced User Experience (Technical Report SS-17-04; 2017 AAAI Spring Symposium Series, p. 6). Association for the Advancement of Artificial Intelligence. https://www.aaai.org/ocs/index.php/SSS/SSS17/paper/viewFile/15363/14575

Yasin, A., Fatima, R., Wen, L., Afzal, W., Azhar, M., & Torkar, R. (2020). On Using Grey Literature and Google Scholar in Systematic Literature Reviews in Software Engineering. IEEE Access, 8, 36226-36243. https://doi.org/10.1109/ACCESS.2020.2971712

Yuan, T. (2023). User Portrait Based on Artificial Intelligence. In J. C. Hung, N. Y. Yen, & J.-W. Chang (Eds.), Frontier Computing (pp. 359-366). Springer Nature. https://doi.org/10.1007/978-981-99-1428-9_44

Zhou, C., Chai, C., Liao, J., Chen, Z., & Shi, J. (2020). Artificial intelligence augmented design iteration support. 2020 13th International Symposium on Computational Intelligence and Design (ISCID), 354-358. https://doi.org/10.1109/ISCID51228.2020.00086

Zhou, J., Tang, Z., Zhao, M., Ge, X., Zhuang, F., Zhou, M., Zou, L., Yang, C., & Xiong, H. (2020). Intelligent Exploration for User Interface Modules of Mobile App with Collective Learning. Proceedings of the 26th ACMSIGKDD International Conference on Knowledge Discovery & Data Mining, 3346-3355. https://doi.org/10.1145/3394486.3403387

Zimmermann, G., Ableitner, T., & Strobbe, C. (2017). User Needs and Wishes in Smart Homes: What Can Artificial Intelligence Contribute? 2017 14th International Symposium on Pervasive Systems, Algorithms and Networks & 2017 11th International Conference on Frontier of Computer Science and Technology & 2017 Third International Symposium of Creative Computing (ISPAN-FCST-ISCC),449-453.https://doi.org/10.1109/ISPAN-FCST-ISCC.2017.66

Chapter 5
Artificial Intelligence in the Industrial Design Process

Introduction

Background

Tools that use artificial intelligence (AI) have recently become popular. For example, Midjourney, Stable Diffusion, and DALL-E 2 are being used to make complex art at breakneck speeds. But AI tools have mostly been used in 2D creative art so far. They could also be useful in industrial design and product development, though.

Industrial design is the process of making new goods, including how they look, how they work, and how they are shaped. Industrial design is an area that is always changing, and new technologies are always being made to help with the design process. With their power to look at data and come up with new ideas, AI tools could completely change how goods are made.

With the help of recent advances in AI, new design tools have been created. These include generative design, which uses algorithms to create new design options based on certain criteria, and computer-aided design, which uses AI to help make and change 3D models. These tools can help with getting ideas, getting inspired, and other parts of the product creation process. This speeds up and improves the design process.

Even though AI could be useful in industrial design, there are also social issues that need to be looked into. Using AI to design products makes people think about the role of human creativity, how AI could replace human workers, and what the moral effects of using AI to design products are.

Boid

Boid is a design shop in Gothenburg that focuses on making gadgets and other physical things. It used to be part of Chalmers, but now it's its own studio that works on both commercial projects and study ones.

Objectives

The goals of the thesis are as follows:

1. To provide an overview of the landscape of AI tools and their potential use in industrial design and product development. This will include an analysis of the strengths and weaknesses of current AI tools and how they can be integrated into the design process to aid in inspiration, ideation, and other stages in product development.
2. To develop an industrial design workflow or model that utilizes the right AI tools to support faster and more creative ideation for physical design and styling. This will include the identification of specific AI tools that can be used to aid in specific stages of the product development process, and the testing of the effectiveness of the proposed workflow.
3. To develop a custom AI model, trained on industrial design imagery, to aid ideation with an industrial design focus. This will include the collection of industrial design imagery and the training of the custom AI model using machine learning and computer vision techniques.
4. To showcase the use of the tools and resulting workflow through a reference project that develops a concept product. This will include the application of the tools and workflow to the design of a specific product, and an evaluation of the effectiveness of the tools and workflow in the design process.
5. To consider the ethical implications of using AI in product development and to suggest best practices for ethical use. This will include an analysis of the potential controversies surrounding the use of AI in product development and the identification of best practices for ethical use of AI in industrial design and product development.
6. To build upon and use the processes and skills taught during the program when it comes to the process of industrial design and the tools for creating and realizing ideas, while incorporating the new elements of using AI to augment the process.

Research Questions

Research Questions:

1. How can the design process be altered to take benefit from the use of AI?
2. What changes must a human make to an AI generated concept in order to create a viable product?

Delimitations

This project will not go into great detail about the systems that AI is based on or how they are made. Also, instead of making its own systems, it will use AI solutions and tools that are already out there to get the job done.

There will be some research done to see if it is possible to train an AI on images of industrial design as part of the project.

Also, the thesis will only quickly talk about AI's more advanced features that aren't covered by the industrial design process.

In order to stay within the time limit, the trial of the new process will also be cut down.

Disposition

First, the report will talk about the background and explain ideas and theories that are important to the thesis. After that, it will talk about the methods that will be used. The method chapter will then be split into two parts. In the first part, we'll talk about how AI can be used in industrial design. In the second part, we'll talk about a "trial run" industrial design job that uses the new method.

Theoretical Background

Artificial Intelligence

In the field of computer science called artificial intelligence (AI), people are working on making machines that are smart enough to do things that usually require human intelligence, like thinking, feeling, and making decisions. AI is done in many ways, but the main types are rule-based systems and neural networks. Rule-based systems use a set of rules to make choices. Expert systems make choices based on what they know about a certain subject. And machine learning, which makes models better over time by using data to do so. Computer vision is the most useful use of AI for this thesis because it lets an AI understand and create pictures.

Because AI has been getting better over the past few years, new design tools have been made, such as generative design and computer-aided design. Generative design uses algorithms to come up with new design choices based on certain criteria. This lets you look at a bigger design space more quickly.

AI's ability to look at data and come up with new ideas is one of its best features in industrial design. AI can help find patterns and trends that can help with the planning process, for example by looking at data about what people like. Artificial intelligence can also be used to model how a product will work, which lets problems be found before the product is actually made.

Even though AI could be useful in industrial design, there are also social issues that need to be thought about. Using AI to design products makes people think about the role of human creativity, how AI could replace human workers, and what the moral effects of using AI to design products are. Additionally, it makes me wonder about the ethics of using other people's artistic work to teach AI models.

Deep Learning

Artificial neural networks (ANNs) are used in deep learning, a branch of machine learning, to learn and describe complex relationships in data. In recent years, this method has become more common because it can automatically pull out and learn features from raw data, so no feature engineering is needed.

Deep learning architectures are made up of many layers of nodes that are all linked to each other. Before passing the data to the next layer, each layer processes and changes it. Usually, a lot of labeled data is used to train these networks. The network learns to make predictions by minimizing a cost function that shows how much its expected output differs from the actual output.

One of the best things about deep learning is that it can work with high-dimensional data, like pictures and sounds, that are hard to show in a simple feature space. Deep learning can also automatically find complex patterns and relationships in data. This makes it very useful for jobs like speech and image recognition, natural language processing, and driving itself.

Computer Vision

Computer vision lets machines read data and figure out what pictures, videos, and other visual media mean. The AI can use this knowledge to either make suggestions or do other things, depending on what it wants to do. It works a lot like human vision. The big difference is that our brains have been trained and linked to context for a lifetime to tell the difference between things we see and figure out what they mean.

The computer needs to be trained before it can be used as part of a vision system. This is usually done with very large datasets that have a lot of pictures or other visual media. These datasets are usually customized to what the AI system's creators want to achieve. Instead of having a person tell the AI what each picture is, algorithms let the system learn to tell the difference between images and what they contain. It is mostly deep learning and convolutional neural networks (CNN) that are used to do this. Deep learning is a type of machine learning in which the methods are based on how the brain processes and learns from a lot of data. This means that, like people, it learns more by doing things over and over again.

Stable Diffusion

A latent diffusion model is a type of deep learning neural network built with likelihood-based models. Stable Diffusion is an AI method for putting together images. It is based on a number of complex partial differential equations that are used to show gaussian noise. Which is a way to basically hide the image in different steps. The AI then does math several times to clear up and get rid of the noise until the equation system is considered "stable." This makes an image that can be seen from prompts or other image data. A lot of pictures that were taken from the internet and put into groups before the training are fed to the AI to train the model. You can do the sorting by hand or with the help of other AI systems. One good thing about stable diffusion models is that they can be used to translate images from one to another. In other words, it can join an uploaded picture and a text prompt to make something. The system is also open source, which means that the community can change it and make it better as study goes on.

DALL-E 2

What is DALL-E? It is an AI that can combine images and it works by storing them in a way called CLIP (Contrastive Language-Image Pre-training). CLIP is used to teach an AI how to connect a picture with a word. This lets the AI understand what an image means and connect words to images that are similar to them in context. A huge amount of data is needed for this, which for DALL-E means about 650 million pictures.

For DALL-E to work, this system has to be run backwards. You can use a separate decoder to go backwards through this process once the AI has been trained to encode and identify context, meaning, and language associations. This lets DALL-E take text input, check it against its huge database of encoded images, and then decode it into an image that fits the text input. [9]

There are also different versions of DALL-E. One of the most important ones is called Craiyon and used to be called DALL-E small.

Midjourney

Midjourney is a product of an independent study lab, and the way it makes images is still a trade secret. When run through a chat program's command line interface, it's very easy for anyone to use. It gives results that are like those from the systems listed in 2.1.3, so it makes sense to think that the models that power it are also similar.

Craiyon

The technology behind Craiyon is similar to that of DALL-E 2, and it used to be known as DALLE Mini. This tool is quick and can make a lot of pictures in a short amount of time, but the quality and accuracy of those pictures are not as good as those made by other tools.

Lexica

Lexica is an easy-to-use online tool for making images that comes with a library. It was probably based on a custom Stable Diffusion model. Because each picture in this database is linked to its own set of parameters, anyone could "reverse engineer" an image and figure out how it was made. This makes the database a good place to learn how to use AI tools.

Prompt Engineering

Because image-based AI depends so much on prompts, which are text-based inputs, being able to make enough of these prompts is essential for getting good results.

Prompt engineering for artificial intelligence (AI) is the process of making sure that the phrases and factors you give the AI to process are optimized and used correctly. This is an important area of research because it can make AI models much more useful and improve their performance. It can also have a big effect on the results they produce, especially those that use language-based inputs.

Users can talk to AI systems more easily and correctly with prompt coding. Users can tell an AI model what they want and what they need by writing clear prompts that use normal language. This makes it easy for the model to understand and respond. This is especially important for tasks like question answering, chatbots, and language translation, where the prompt quality can have a big effect on how accurate, useful, and high-quality the AI-generated answer or picture is.

One more good thing about rapid engineering is that it can help fix the problem of bias in AI models. By making sure that the language and design of the prompts are fair and neutral, developers can lower the chance that harmful stereotypes and mistakes in the training data will be spread. Also, prompt engineering can be added to current methods for reducing bias, like data pre-processing and model regularization, to make AI systems even more fair and open to everyone.

For prompt engineering to work, researchers and writers need to know a lot about technology, like how to use natural language processing, machine learning, and software engineering. They also need to know a lot about the specific application area and the people who will be using the AI system. They also need to be able to try and improve their prompt design over and over again to make sure it gives them accurate and reliable results. AI is becoming more and more important to society and progress, so quick engineering will become an even more important skill for experts, developers, and people who work in the field.

Dreambooth

Creating large text-to-image models is a big step forward in artificial intelligence. They make it possible to make high-quality, varied images from textual cues. But these kinds of models often can't perfectly copy the way people look in a certain example and make new versions of them for different situations.

Dreambooth is a way to make text-to-image spread models more unique. By giving Dreambooth a few pictures of a subject or idea it wants to learn about, it can fine-tune a text-to-image model that has already been trained, like Stable Diffusion, to learn how to connect a unique word or phrase with that topic. This embedding makes it possible to make new photorealistic pictures of the subject, which can then be put in scenes, poses, views, and lighting conditions that aren't in the reference images. Dreambooth training lets the model do this while keeping the most important parts of the learned subject or topic.

ControlNet

ControlNet is a method made for Text-to-image diffusion models that gives the user more control over the images that are made. It does its job by adding itself to the building blocks of an AI model's neural network. These blocks are different parts of the program that do different things, like computer vision and making images.

ControlNet gives the user more ways to add information, like sketches, edge maps, depth maps, and normal maps, so they can make images with more precision. Existing diffusion models are used as building blocks for the system, which is taught on the inputs listed above to get the best results. In the field of industrial design, one example could be rendering an image with normal maps that can be seen and then using this image to quickly try out different materials and surface styles using Stable Diffusion.

It also opens the door for AI and designers to work together more, since ControlNet lets Stable Diffusion correctly understand and make pictures from the designer's sketches.

Breadboard

The media browser Breadboard was made to work with AI-generated material, which makes it a useful tool for this thesis. Due to the large number of images that AI tools can create very quickly, it is important to have a way to watch, organize, and look over these images. The breadboard lets pictures be automatically imported into the software and lets the user quickly see the settings that were used to make the images. This is very important when you want to make images that look the same and have full control over the generation process.

When you need to choose pictures based on certain qualities or design elements, being able to tag and organize them becomes very important. The search tool in Breadboard also lets you look for images based on the prompts that were used to make them.

Industrial Design

Industrial design is the process of coming up with new goods for production, including how they look, how they work, and how they are made. Design, engineering, and marketing are all used together in this multidisciplinary area to make products that are useful and look good. The goal of industrial design is to make useful things that are also nice to look at, easy to use, and perfect for people's needs. Industrial design usually involves study, coming up with ideas, making prototypes, testing them, and then making the final product. In this step, industrial designers learn about what people want, how the market is changing, and what new tools they can use in the design process. Designers make the first sketches and models of the product during the concept development process. The design is tweaked and a physical model of the product is often made during the prototyping process. After the final design is made, it is tried to make sure it meets safety and performance standards. Only then is it made in large quantities.

New technologies and materials are always being made, so industrial design is an area that is always changing. Sustainable design, which means making products that are good for the earth and use long-lasting materials, has become more popular over the past few years.

The Design Process

Design Thinking

Design thinking is a way of solving problems that focuses on people. It includes understanding users' needs and points of view, coming up with new ideas, making prototypes, and testing these solutions. It was first made by the design company IDEO in the 1990s, and since then, many businesses, both public and private, have used it as a way to come up with new ideas.

Design thinking theories and methods usually have five steps: understand, describe, come up with ideas, make a prototype, and test it. During this step, you study and observe the user to get a sense of what they want and need. A point of view and the problem are set up in the describe step. During the ideate stage, techniques like brainstorming and idea generation are used to come up with a number of possible answers.

During the prototype stage, a physical or digital version of the answer is made so that the idea can be tested and improved. Lastly, the sample is looked at and made better based on what users said during testing.

Design thinking can be used to solve many different kinds of problems, from creating new businesses and ways of running organizations to making goods and services. It's different because it focuses on trying things out and doing them again and again. This lets you quickly learn about different methods and try them out.

To sum up, design thinking gives you a way to come up with new ideas by making sure you fully understand users and their wants. This means that design thinking can help businesses solve tough problems, grow, and be more successful by using a structured method and putting people first.

Design Thinking Bootleg

Bootleg is a set of tools and methods created by designers, teachers, and students from all over the world. It shows how to build something and what steps you should take during that process. There are five "modes" in Bootleg, which represent the different stages of a design job. The five steps are Test, Define, Empathize, and Ideate.

Building respect for the end user is what human-centered design is all about. To do this, you have to observe, interact with, and become fully immersed in the users' experiences.

Define is the step in the process where you turn what you learned in the empathy stage into specific needs and requirements that help you define the project and understand the problem.

Ideate is the point where the process starts to become more real. This is the beginning of looking into many different ideas. The goal is to make a large space of possible answers that are both many and different.

In the Prototype stage, ideas are tested to see if they are possible. Making real and digital prototypes that the user can interact with lets you see how they react and feel about them, which helps you figure out how the user experiences the product.

During testing, feedback is gathered and used to improve the answer based on what users say. Testing is very repetitive because the results you get may mean you need to go back and make the result even better.

Method

Literature review

There will be a literature study to look at the world of AI and find out which AIs are useful for industrial design and how they work. The review will also look at how designs are made now to find places where AI can be used in the process. A literature review will help you find and outline important articles and pieces of information that will help you build your understanding of the process.

The way we look for relevant literature had to change a little because artificial intelligence is an area that is growing quickly. It wasn't important to find well-known peer-reviewed pieces in the field; instead, it was important to find the newest and most relevant studies and research on the subject. This makes it more important to use up-to-date knowledge and make sure the thesis is in line with the most recent changes in the field.

Boid Design Process

Figure 1. Boid Process

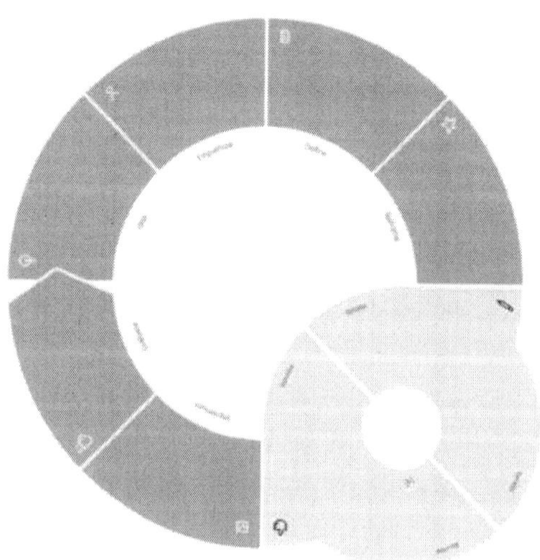

The Boid design method is a version of design thinking that is used at Boid, but with some changes.

This is the main process that this thesis will look at, and the method or process will be made to fit this process. Figure 1 shows the Boid process.

AI Process Development

Since the project's goal is to use AI tools in the industrial design process, this part of the thesis will look at the different AI tools that are out there and figure out what makes them possible for the process. The thesis will also talk about what factors in these tools are important for the outcome and finally pick one or more AI tools to move on to the trial project stage.

AI Evaluation

A list of criteria will be made, and a few picked AI tools will be judged on them in order to find the best one for the job. All of the tools will use the same questions so that the images made by AI are all the same.

The criteria used for evaluating image-based AI tools are as follows.

1. **Image quality**: The quality of generated images is a crucial factor in evaluating image generation models. This includes factors such as image resolution, sharpness, and realism.
2. **Diversity and novelty**: The ability of a model to generate a diverse and novel set of images can indicate its creative potential. This relates directly to being able to use the AI generated images as inspiration.
3. **Consistency and coherence**: An image generation model should produce consistent and coherent images, meaning that the AI should consistently produce acceptable results.
4. **Computational efficiency**: The speed and resource usage of a model is an important factor, as this can impact its practical use.
5. **Generalization**: The ability of a model to generate images beyond its training data is important in evaluating its robustness and generalization.
6. **User control**: The level of user control over the generated images is a consideration. This includes control over factors such CFG, guidance scale and other quality parameters.
7. **Robustness to input**: The ability of a model to handle diverse and complex input, such as text or images, is a key factor in evaluating its practical use.
8. **Accessibility and usability**: The ease of use and accessibility of an image generation model is important. This means barriers of entry and how easy the UI is to interact with.

AI Selection

Based on the list made in the previous step, various AI tools will be evaluated and given the best place in Boid's creation process.

AI training

One of the goals of this thesis is to make and improve an AI model that focuses on industrial design and making images that are useful for the design process. This will help current AI tools that make images work better with design tasks. Because making an AI model is hard, this goal will mostly be reached with tools and software that already exist.

LoRA

LoRA, which stands for "Low rank adaptation," is a way to fine-tune Stable Diffusion models by giving the software training pictures and the captions that go with them, kind of like how Dreambooth works. The user can "bias" the Stable Diffusion Model toward the pictures that are given. It will be used to make Stable Diffusion work better with images of industrial design in this case.

The good thing about LoRA over Dreambooth is that it doesn't need as much time or computer power. With LoRA, training a model can be done in a few hours instead of days with other tools like Dreambooth.

Kohya WebUI

The coder bmaltais made Kohya WebUI, a graphical user interface that makes it easy to use the Stable Diffusion training scripts. Dreambooth is one of the training methods that can be used, but LoRA training is the most useful for this job.

Ideation

The way ideas are generated for this project will be a little different from how ideas are generated for most industrial design products. Common methods like drawing, moodboards, and brainstorming will be mixed with photo synthesizing generative AI tools to increase the number of concepts and ideas that are available and to help develop these concepts further.

Moodboard

A moodboard is a picture that helps you show what style and look you want for the finished result. It usually has things like colors, materials, pictures, and words that are put together in a collage style so that they are easy to see. By making a mood board, artists can clearly explain the idea behind their design and make decisions about things like colors, materials, and finishes. For this thesis, the moodboard might be a little different from the norm because it includes parts that were made by AI.

Brainstorming

The method of brainstorming is all about coming up with a lot of different concepts, ideas, and answers quickly and without any other constraints. With this way, you can explore and build on any idea without worrying about being turned down, so don't be too harsh on ideas. The best thing about this process is that it is completely unplanned, which often leads to new ideas and concepts that might not have been possible in a more controlled setting. It's then possible to evaluate these ideas and decide whether to use some or all of them in the end product.

Sketching

The main way to visualize and improve the ideas that are created will be through sketching. In order to make it easier to share the ideas with partners and other important people, and also to help people understand the ideas better, this is done. There will be both paper and computer sketches made for this project.

Specification of Requirements

When you do study or get information from the client, you fill out a document called a specification of requirements. By making a list of specific, clear requirements, you can lay the groundwork for the project and know exactly what it needs to do, all without having to come up with ideas first. As soon as ideas start to come up, they are carefully checked against the standards to see if they are workable.

Concept Selection

For this project, choosing a concept will be done in full cooperation with the company, which will be the client for this thesis. This means that Boid will give feedback on the concepts that are shown and will eventually decide which parts of the design and aspects will be used in the final concept of the trial process.

3D Modeling

Three-dimensional modeling (3D modeling) will be used to accurately show the end product's sizes, shapes, and designs. Rhinoceros 7 will be used only for this project.

Rendering

Several renders will be made with KeyShot to get a good idea of what the final result of the trial project will look like. The goal of these is to accurately show the end project's shape and material and to make appealing pictures that best show the design and functionality of the chosen idea.

Implementation and Results

Literature Study

Consumer reactions to AI design: Exploring consumer willingness to pay for AI-designed products.

It says that AI is "a system's ability to correctly interpret external data, to learn from such data, and to use those learnings to achieve specific goals and tasks through flexible adaptation."

As a business tool, some people are trying to use "AI designed." AI can design goods by guessing what people will want and how they will act, which lowers the risk and cost of coming up with new ideas. Which could change the way products are designed in a big way.

But people are better at understanding what customers really want, which is something AI has trouble with in the past. People often say that AI is more logical and rational when it comes to design. This could be both a strength and a weakness, since AI doesn't take into account the emotional and human parts of design. In the idea generation stage, for example, human thinkers can get stuck when they are faced with a lot of data. AI algorithms, on the other hand, can make predictions and come up with ideas that humans might not notice. When people are trying to come up with new ideas, they always have a bias. AI can help when it comes to screening ideas.

AI is strongly linked to new things that people find interesting. More variety can often make people more interested in a product, which makes them want to learn more about it. So, as people learn more about AI in general, goods that say "AI Designed" might not seem as new or interesting to them.

> "When consumer knowledge is low, consumer willingness to pay is higherfor AI-designed products than for professional-designed products; curiosity mediates the path from the design source to the willingness to pay. However, when consumer knowledge is high, the willingness to pay for AI-designed products is attenuated; curiosity does not play a mediating role"

The chapter backs up the idea that people are more likely to pay more for goods that were made by AI. It also proves that this is because I'm interested. But this study doesn't look at things like how people see quality, meaning, or the beauty of the design. In simple terms, this means that a lot of very important factors in industrial design are not looked into.

The study also proved that people are less willing to pay for AI Design when they know more about it. The study also discovered that people are more ready to pay for products that were made by humans than those that were made by AI.

In Search of Design Inspiration: A Semantic-Based Approach: Special Issue on Artificial Intelligence in Design

This chapter is part of the EU-funded TRENDS project, which aims to create a software tool that helps with the ideation step of design. This chapter specifically looks at how the affects have changed the design of cars.

This chapter takes a different look at how AI can be used in industrial design. Instead of making their own images, the researchers use a tool called OntoTag, which is a method for retrieving images based on their meaning. That is, the experts don't make new images; instead, they use images that already exist. OntoTag was made just for designers. It uses algorithms and language and phrases that are special to designers to store and find information that designers need.

Researchers found that designers often use certain words or phrases to "anchor" their looks for ideas in a certain area. For example, "cars" + futuristic + colorful.

They also found a link between the level of abstraction and the level of creativity in design. Which lets the researchers guess if "diffuse" AI imagery, rather than fully generated pictures, is a better way to get ideas. This is because artists often get ideas from data that has nothing to do with the field they are working in.

The chapter also talks about the idea that individual style is important to both designers and artists. Because AI often gives very concrete pictures of possible ideas, it could be hard or take some time to get used to using it as motivation. AI might not be a tool that works for everyone in the planning process because it is very personal.

When a designer is looking for ideas, they might want to find pictures that show abstract ideas instead of detailed details. Basically: picture retrieval based on meaning.

In conclusion, AI can help in the very early stages of product development by making tools that let the creator get ideas from more general ideas. To put it simply, AI can help users make moodboards and trendboards that can spark ideas.

Explaining Artificial Intelligence Generation and Creativity

Before we can understand what creativity means in terms of AI, this chapter tries to explain what creativity means in humans. The study says that people are creative by association most of the time. People are able to come up with new ideas that often meet the standards for being creative by putting together different, often unrelated ideas.

People often think that being creative is something that only humans can do, but AI is becoming more and more important in the creative process, both on its own and as a tool for artists. The goal of this chapter is to explain AI in creative areas.

The chapter finds that DALL-E 2, an AI that creates images, seems to meet the standards for general creativity. It then goes on to explain that Creative AI is different because novelty is so important. A lot of the time, creative AI is set to expand instead of interpolate. This means that they look beyond their training and "take inspiration" from it instead of putting together a result from the data they have access to. The goal is to make something new and different by putting together "ingredients" that have never been put together before.

The chapter also talks about the need to build trust between people and AI, and it is thought that XAI (Explainable Artificial Intelligence) will be a big part of this. AI systems are very complicated, so most people who use them don't really understand how they work or how they get and use their data. This makes people unsure of and possibly suspicious of the results that artificial intelligence gives them.

The Quest for AI Creativity

This chapter from IBM talks about what creativity means to them and how it links to AI based on their own experiences and research.

Generative models are often used to build AI that can synthesize images. These models work by copying the data they were taught on. When you change the parameters or vectors, you can get "new" results that are like the data it was learned on. There is still no clear definition of creativity, but it usually means coming up with something new, surprising, and useful. That being said, AI can easily think of something new on its own. But it's hard to think of something new, useful, and out of the ordinary.

The chapter makes the case that parameters can point an AI in the right direction. It also asks if it is possible to teach it to create on its own and if it can understand what is truly beautiful. The next part of the chapter talks about how we can teach AI to understand what is beautiful, but it might be hard to get it to make something beautiful from scratch. How people learn to be creative is different from how computers learn to be creative.

Then IBM says that they are not trying to remake the human mind. Instead, they are making systems that work with people to help them be more creative and come up with new ideas more often. AI can also help with less exciting parts of the artistic process. Like going through hours of video or choosing pictures.

The chapter talks a lot about AI creation, but it also stresses how important the "human soul/touch" is in creative work.

The Role of Artificial Intelligence in Achieving the Sustainable Development Goals

The SDGs were set by the UN, and this part talks about what role artificial intelligence might play in meeting them. It also talks about the possible effects, both good and bad, that AI might have on sustainability.

As part of the SDGs, one of the biggest issues AI has to deal with is the fact that by 2030, IT will use up to 20% of the world's energy. A lot of electricity is used by the datacenters that are needed to run and operate such high-tech equipment. Finally, this makes it clear how important it is to find and develop green energy sources to power our new AIs.

AI is often shaped by the needs and ideals of the country where it is created. This means that if it is used in other parts of the world where the culture and way of thinking are very different, it could lead to problems.

The social credit system used in China is an example of how AI has been used to divide people. Which looks at details about how people live and could have very bad effects. It could also make the gap between people who can buy AI and people who can't get bigger.

AI is naturally skewed because of the information it learns, so it could be discriminating against women and minorities without even realizing it. Aside from that, the media it learns from could give it social views. Since technology usually helps people with more education, AI could make inequality worse. This means that low- to middle-income countries might fall even further behind because they might not be able to pay the systems that high-income countries put in place.

Evaluation of Available image-based AI

It was possible to test the different models by giving each one a set of three questions to answer. All models used the same prompt so that the rating would be the same. There were a minimum of four pictures that each AI had to make, which were then used to judge the models.

The three prompts created to evaluate the different tools were:

1. "A futuristic and sleek small digital camera, with a simplistic and minimalistic design, Product photography, behance, pinterest design, light background"
2. "A tabletop dishwasher with a clean and modern design, soft curves, grey, black and white materials. octane render, 8k, bright background"
3. "A portable gaming console with a touch screen and forest green highlights, product design sketch, visible brushstrokes, greg Rutkowski"

Midjourney

Figure 2. Midjourney Images

1. Midjourney produces some of the best AI generated images currently. While the results may at times appear a bit "painterly"
2. Midjourney has been one of the most consistent in being able to produce diverse and novel ideas, often being able to create "new" concepts.
3. Midjourney's quality is consistent, and the images produced are almost always coherent.
4. Midjourney can be quite slow at times, depending on the load on the network and other factors.
5. Midjourney appear to be one of the best in terms of generating images that hold little to no resemblance to the images you might imagine it's been trained on.

6. User control is vast, If a bit complicated. It's able to take a variety of parameters to modify the end result.
7. Midjourney handles a variety of inputs and is often able to create usable results.
8. Midjourney runs through a command prompt interface through discord, which can be convoluted and difficult to use in some cases.

Stable Diffusion

Figure 3. Stable Diffusion Images

1. The quality of images can vary, but in general the results are good and usable. It does however fail in the third test. Resolution and aspect ratio is adjustable.
2. With manipulation of the CFG scale you can produce quite novel results with the trade-off of lower quality and vice versa. It doesn't like to stray form training material in some cases.
3. Consistency varies depending on the subject. In the example of the camera, a lot of generations had to be run in order to produce coherent images where the perspective and lens wasn't skewed.
4. Speed is the main advantage of local. Run on a Nvidia RTX 3080, it produces results faster than any other of the tested options.
5. The model of stable diffusion run for these tests tends to have some issues when it comes to producing "new" results. Using an image input and setting the CFG scale high can alleviate these problems slightly.
6. Local stable diffusion offers by far the most control of input and output with a variety of different parameters.
7. Handles both text and image input well.
8. While the UI offers a lot of options, it is easy to navigate and use without much prior experience.

DALLE - 2

Figure 4. DALL-E 2 Images

1. The image quality varies heavily from prompt to prompt. It often leans towards more "photographic" results, but often creates broken images with elements that overlap and make little sense. It also struggles when asked to produce sketches.
2. While DALLE has proven capable of creating interesting shapes, it's lacking in terms of detail when creating concepts for design
3. Consistency is lacking and the coherence of images in these cases vary wildly. With some being great images while order is bland or unreadable at times.
4. DALLE is quite fast, with no real major complaints.
5. DALLE seems to struggle in creating design concepts that create "new" features and inspiration
6. User control is good; the UI is good, and it provides the user with control over the guidance scale.
7. DALLE takes both text and image input.
8. Since DALLE runs on its own website, the UI is tailored for it and allows for easy adjustments.

Lexica

Figure 5. Lexica Images

1. Lexica is one of the top contenders for image quality and produces a unique style of images most of the time.
2. While the images are of high quality, novelty can sometimes be a bit lacking.
3. Lexica produces incredibly consistent, high-quality results that almost always form a coherent image without major artifacts and errors.
4. Lexica works very fast, no complaints regarding the speed of generation.
5. Lexica appears to be a bit held back by its training material in some cases, but it generally doesn't prove to be a major issue.
6. Provides the user with control of what model to use and the guidance scale. Also has resolution and aspect ratio options.
7. Does not take image input but handles text input very well.

Lexica uses its own website with very simple UI that is easy to use even for beginners.

8. Lexica runs from its own website and provides the user with control over the prompt, negative prompt, resolution, and guidance scale.

Craiyon

Figure 6. Craiyon Images

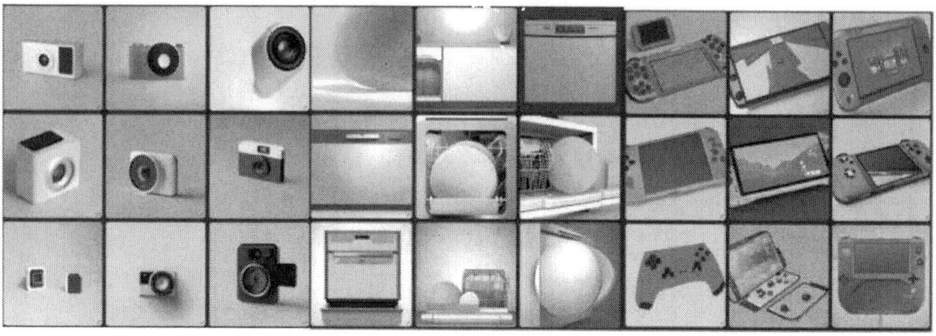

1. Quality of images can be quite lacklustre, resolution quite small.
2. While the images generated are quite simple, it often provides a good amount of variety since it produces 9 images per prompt. These 9 often vary a lot in form and design.
3. Consistency is quite low, as it seems to be very dependent on the prompt, it struggles with certain styles and products. See test 2 for example.
4. On the lower end of the scale in terms of speed, but nothing too dramatic.
5. Craiyon seems to struggle with producing generalized images that remain coherent in certain areas. See test 2 and 3.
6. Craiyon is very simple in terms of control and only offers control of the prompt. No guidance scale or resolution.
7. Craiyon only takes text input.
8. Extremely easy to use as there is essentially only a textbox.

AI Selection

The main tool for developing the process was decided to be stable diffusion, mostly because of what Boid said and the evaluations that were done. Because Stable Diffusion is free software that can be run locally, it wasn't picked because it needs expensive gear or data centers. It can also be made better all the time by adding plugins and changing the exact factors that affect how images are made. The designer has a lot more power over the process and the end result because of this.

Design Process and AI

For this process development, artificial intelligence was used as a tool instead of a full replacement for the designer. This was done to test and learn how the individual designer affects the final product and what changes a designer needs to make to an AI-generated idea in order to make a live final product.

We can also see from the literature review that AI tools often have some bias built in, which hopefully can be fixed by having a creator step in and make changes.

Process Development

Process Outline

As a way to see what artificial intelligence could really do in the routine, the first draft of the process used AI tools in the "maximalist" way. Figure 7 shows this first draft.

Figure 7. Initial Process Draft

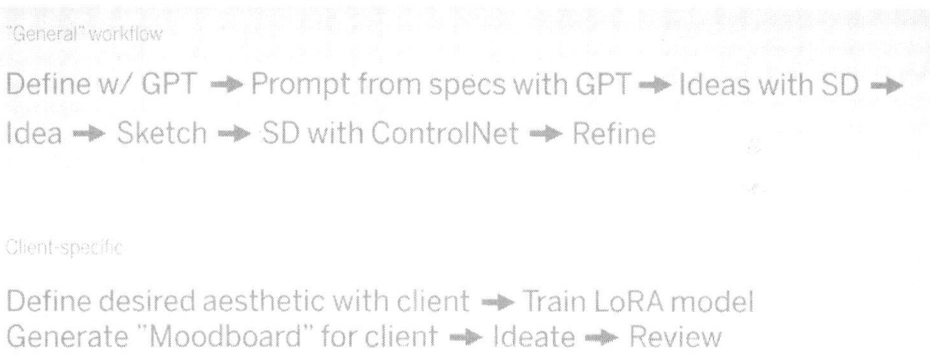

This process was found to be flawed after more thought and talk with Boid. It doesn't take into account client specifications and requirements, ideation loops, or manual refinement.

After hearing this, the process was taken back to the drawing board to be made better. The process would be based on the strengths of the AI tools that were picked and made available. This was ideation. With design thought as a starting point, people talked about how to find the best tools for each step of the process. After that, these steps were quickly tested with their corresponding tools for each part of the process to see if it was possible. Then it occurred to split the process into two main parts: the first part would be to define the project and make the first images; the second part would be to turn the information and images into a real idea, which would then be improved until it became a final idea. Because the process isn't linear and allows for iteration and ideation, an iteration loop was put in the middle of these two main parts. The process that came out of this can be seen, and 4.5 goes into more detail about it.

AI Training

It was the goal of the AI training to make a model that tilts the output of Stable Diffusion toward product design. At its core, Stable Diffusion has trouble making designs that look good and doesn't understand surfaces or design features. In order to fix this, three models were made with the help of LoRA. Pictures from the internet were used to show a lot of different design features, shapes, styles, and materials. The pieces were put together by hand based on the author's preferences and emphasized modern and current design. Some unique tags were added to each picture so that all of the training material could be called up at the same time. All of the general product images were marked with "HUID2" or a phrase that meant the same thing based on the model. In this way, we can use any of the trained pictures during the prompting. All of the items were marked with the word "HUIDMAT" and a certain keyword. This key word would be "KeyAnodifedBlack" for black anodized aluminum.

All the pictures were resized to 512x512 pixels and given their own titles to help the AI understand what they showed. This way, parts of these pictures could be used to make new pictures. In figure 8, you can see some of the pictures that were used to teach the models.

Figure 8. Selection of AI Training Material

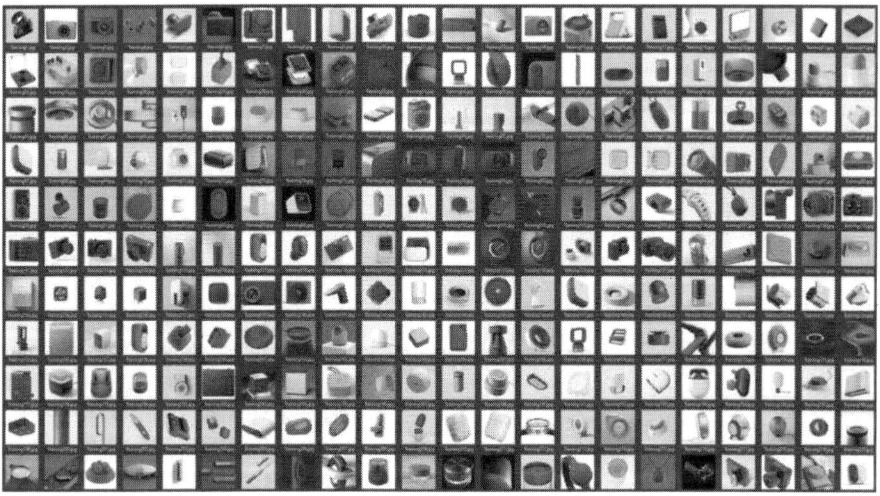

HUGTRTESTI

The first test model made was HGTRTEST1. The purpose of this model was to find out if teaching AI was a good way to fix the problem of Stable Diffusion not understanding design.

According to 4.2.2, 22 pictures were collected and set up. This model went through 100 training steps for each picture, and the whole process took about an hour.

Results from the model looked good; they showed that Stable Diffusion could immediately spot and use design elements like surfaces, shapes, and split lines better. The model did have trouble making whole products, though. It would often just mix different shapes and parts together, making results that were impossible to understand. It also had trouble cutting pictures and showing small details. The small sample was a big problem for the model, but that was fixed in the next model. You can see some examples of the model in figure 9.

Figure 9. HUGTRTESTI Sample

HUIDI

The goal of HUID1 was to make the model work better overall and fix problems caused by the small sample used in HUGTRTEST1. There are now 142 pictures in the dataset instead of 22. The teaching process, which still had 100 steps and captioned pictures, was the same other than that. For this model, the whole training process took about 2.5 hours. It was clear that this model was better than HGTRTEST1 because it could easily and regularly make images that looked like product renders. It can make it easy to tell the difference between product parts and combine different design elements.

It did have trouble with small details like buttons and dials, though, and didn't know where to put these different tasks or how to fit them into the picture. You can see some examples of the model in figure 10.

Figure 10. HUID1 Sample Images

HUID2

HUID2 was an attempt to make a final model that was much more powerful and could re-create and use a wider range of design elements than the first model could. It was also meant to make the model better at adding different materials and patterns. This was made possible by adding 500 new pictures of goods, textures, and materials to the dataset. The training method stayed the same, but the captions of the pictures were slightly changed so that certain materials and textures could be used when the pictures were being made.

There were 100 training steps for each picture, which added up to almost 7 hours of training for HUID2. The model can make results that are even more consistently coherent and create a wider range of design features. This is great for getting ideas, but it could make it harder to get the exact results you want. It also gives up some interesting small features to make the picture look better. HUID1 is better than it when it comes to rendering tiny details, though. Figure 11 shows some pics from the model that show what it looks like.

Figure 11. HUID2 Sample Images

Prompt Creation

To get the most out of Stable Diffusion, you need to organize your prompts in a certain way and think about a few things. In stable diffusion, the prompts are put in a priority order. This means that the image generation will use the order in which the words are entered to decide which ones are most important. Making sure that the item we want to make comes early in the sequence increases our chances of getting results that we can use. A good way to start coming up with a camera idea would be to say something like, "A modern camera with lens attached."

Using brackets is another way to either get around the ranking order or improve it. The importance is shown by the number of brackets. We use: ((A modern camera with lens attached)) to tell you more about it since the camera is the most important part of this question.

It is generally better for Stable Diffusion to work with more specific prompts, so giving it a wider range of attributes to work with will usually lead to images with more detail and accuracy. These are the words we add to the prompt in this case: "with shutter button, with charging dock for file transfer and charging of the device, Sony, small and light."

After that, we choose the image's style. To make sure that the pictures we make are product renders, we add keywords. Here, keywords are pretty open-ended, but using words that are often associated with high-quality pictures, like "8k," makes sure that the quality is more consistent. Right now, these words were picked: "product render, 8 k, sharp focus, white background."

We use specific language because we are going to use a custom-trained model of Stable Diffusion. You need to type "<lora:HUID2:1>" in order for the model to load. The model's weight is given by the number that comes after the colon. The word "HUID2" is also used in the prompt to bring up all the training information. Putting it all together gives us a question like this:

> "((A modern camera with lens attached)), with shutter button, with charging dock for file transfer and charging of the device, sony, compact and lightweight,HUID2, matte, (HUID2), product render, 8k, <lora:HUID2:0.8>, sharp focus, white background"

In order to remove potentially undesirable attributes from appearing in the images we also use a negative prompt. These are generally much simpler and takes the form of a list with words for the AI to avoid. All generations during this thesis uses the same set of negative prompts which are:

"deformed, bad proportions, unrealistic, fantasy, out of frame, out of focus, cropped, bad product, not centered, incomplete, sketch, drawing, ugly, overexposed, underexposed, unrealistic, wood"

Trial Project

With help from Boid, a certain product was picked to test the process on. A compact camera was the item picked. The trial project's purpose was to make sure the process works as planned and find places where it might need to be improved.

Resulting Process, AI Industrial Design Workflow

Working together with Boid, the process is being made based on their suggestions and experiences. Along with other well-known methods and ideas, like Design Thinking, this is what the process is built on. A lot of attention is paid to the ideation stage and later stages of the process because that's where AI tools are thought to have the most effect, given the current Boid process and AI tools that are available. There are six steps in the process, but like many design processes, it is not straight and has a lot of iteration loops and turns to make changes and improvements. A graphic version that is easy to read has also been made and can be found in figure 12. The six steps are shown below.

Define

The next steps will build on what was done in this step. It reminds me a lot of the empathize and define steps of design thinking. This is where we talk to the client and the people and get the information we need. Here, we also try to find out things like what the client wants in terms of style, what items are already on the market, and what their needs are. With this knowledge in mind, we can begin to use AI tools. With Kohya WebUI and LoRa models' help, we can train a model that creates images in a way that is specific to the project. If this path for training is picked, the model could be used as a guide for the next steps.

Prompt

This is where AI tools are first used, in the Prompt stage. We can start coming up with ideas using the project outline we made in the last step. We can make pictures in Stable Diffusion by making questions that really show what the client and user want. The point of making these pictures is to get ideas and get a feel for what the final result might look like. It is possible to speed up this step of the process by using prompt templates that have already been made. In the case of product design, prompts often have a lot of the same ones. This is because questions often cover the same things.

Evaluate

We can begin to evaluate the images that were made in the Prompt step. Using a program called Breadboard can make the process of labeling and sorting the pictures go much faster. Get rid of pictures that don't show important design and attribute elements, and then tag the elements you want to show. For the product in question, these pictures will be used as ideas and as a customized moodboard. It's also important to think about whether or not these design aspects can actually be designed and made. As the ideas and themes get better, we will go back to this stage to get more ideas.

Iterate

From the Evaluate stage to the Refine stage, the Iterate stage is in the middle. The major goals of this stage are to test, confirm, iterate, and confirm the results from the Evaluate and Refine stages. Another important thing that this stage is for is to make sure that the project stays on track by using client feedback. This early in the process makes it more likely that the client's needs and wants will be met, and it also lowers the chance that changes will need to be made later on.

Refine

Now that our AI-generated pictures are in order, we can start coming up with ideas and making them better. With the help of ControlNet, we will make sketches and/or simple 3D models that we will then feed into Stable Diffusion. This will help us learn more about the ideas that might be interesting by keeping the proposed ideas' shape and lines. This can also help the artist get ahead of the CMF process because they can try out different materials before choosing one. Right now is also a good time to use the simple 3D models to check the shape and usability. By improving these parts at this time, the project risk is lowered, and these parts can be iterated and made better if needed. We can go back to the Evaluate stage and use what we've learned here along with feedback from clients and users to make the results even better, more solid, and more reliable.

Clarify

The last changes are made at this point in the process. This is where the final sketches would be made, and the ideas and pictures would be improved. Within this stage, the goal is to prepare the ideas to be shown to the client. The process goes on to its last step if the client agrees with the idea.

Finalize

Now that the idea has been accepted, the focus shifts to finishing the project. This means making the CAD models, drawings, and maybe even prototypes that can be built. At this point in the project, all the big problems should have been fixed during the Evaluate, Iterate, and Refine stages. This means that there shouldn't be many chances or iterations at this point. Stable Diffusion with ControlNet lets the designer try out different materials while working in CAD. This helps them decide on the final CMF specs of the product.

Figure 12. Developed Process

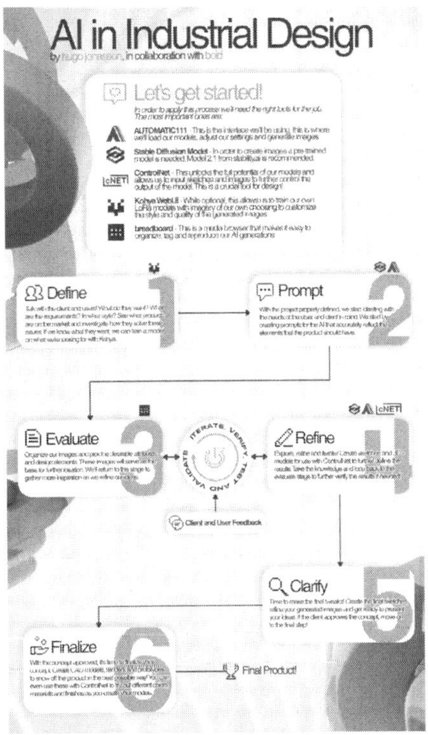

Trial Project Implementation

Define

In order to get the trial project done in the time allotted, the define stage was cut short and study was sped up. Together with Boid, the product specs were chosen, which laid the groundwork for the prompting process. The specs came from cameras that are already on the market and from the author and Boid's combined photography experience.

It was chosen that a Sony camera would be the test product. In Table 1, you can see the details.

This project also chose to use all three models that were made for this thesis. This meant that HGTRTEST1, HUID1, and HUID2 were all used, with HUID2 being used the most during the process.

Table 1. Concept Specifications

Full Frame 35mm sensor	**Rear Screen**	**Rear Main Dial**
Rear Thumb Dial	Shutter Button	Ergonomic Grip
Function Buttons	Custom Setting Buttons	Thread Mount
Solid Metal Frame	Medium size form-factor	Thin Body
Sony FE Mount	Interchangeable Lenses	SD Card Slot
Flash	Built in AI filters	LIDAR Sensor

Prompt

The prompts used are presented in table 2.

Table 2. Stable Diffusion Prompt

"((A modern camera with lens attached)), with shutter button, with charging dock for file transfer and charging of the device, sony, compact and lightweight,HUID2, matte, (HUID2), product render, 8k, <lora:HUID2:0.8>, sharp focus, white background"
"((A modern camera with lens attached)), sony, compact and lightweight,HUID2, black aluminium, led, device (HUID2), product render, 8k, <lora:HUID2:0.8>, sharp focus, white background"

In conjunction with these, the set of negative prompts previously defined were also utilized. Table 3, Negative prompts.

"deformed, bad proportions, unrealistic, fantasy, out of frame, out of focus, cropped, bad product, not centered, incomplete, sketch, drawing, ugly, overexposed, underexposed, unrealistic, wood"

Evaluate I

Using the prompts described in the last section, the first step of the evaluation involved making pictures with and without sketches. Sketches ranged from being just rough ideas to being fully formed drawings. This kind of sketching can be seen in Figures 13 and 14. The goal was to see how well ControlNet handles sketches with different levels of depth and how fast the process could be by using simple sketches to come up with ideas. The AI made a lot of pictures that couldn't be understood, so the images were put into groups based on how relevant they were to the project. These were taken out of the report. Figures 15 and 16 show the pictures that were picked for this step.

Figure 13. Sketches Example

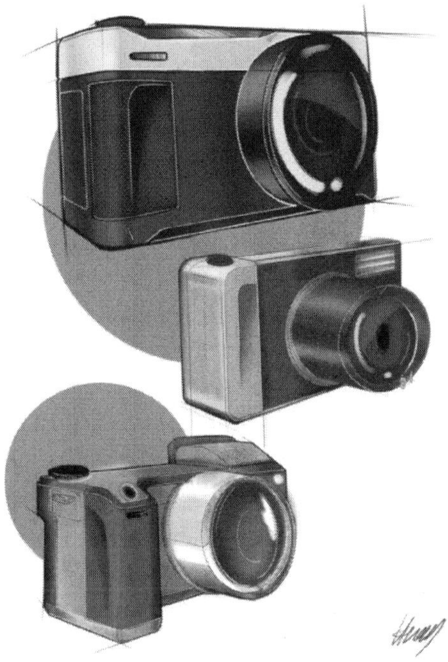

Figure 14. Sketch Example 2

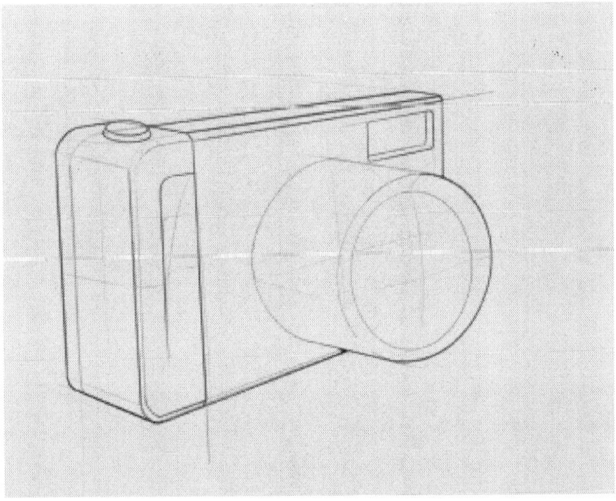

Figure 15. Evaluate 1, Generated Images

Figure 16. Evealuate 1, Generated Images 2

Iterate

The sketches and pictures that were made were shown to the designers at Boid, who gave the project good feedback. The images and sketches that were made did use AI, but they thought that the product itself could look less like a normal camera to make it stand out as something that was created with AI. With this feedback in mind, the work went on to find even stranger shapes and functions, which were then put back into the AI to help it come up with more ideas for the next version of the camera.

The AI did come up with a lot of pictures that could have given the project a lot of design ideas, but it was clear right away that the AI often can't take into account how the function works. How the buttons are laid out and placed, as well as the dials, are all examples of usability. To fix this problem with the AI, a "function-board" was made to make it easier to keep track of all the features that needed to be added and show how they could be used. Figure 17 shows this board.

Figure 17. Function Board

Evaluate 2

Put some pictures next to the sketches on the screen. Show pictures that gave you ideas.

Keep the Boid comments and the product's functions in mind as you continue working on it. Try out different shapes, design elements, and form factors. ControlNET could be used to turn pencil sketches into pictures by making a bunch of loose sketches that showed these ideas. Figures 18 and 19 show these sketches. From that point on, the generations were looked at, sketches were made, and these sketches were fed back into the AI until a rough idea of the end idea was found. Figure 20 shows the AI generations that were chosen for this step.

Figure 18. Concept Sketches for ControlNet

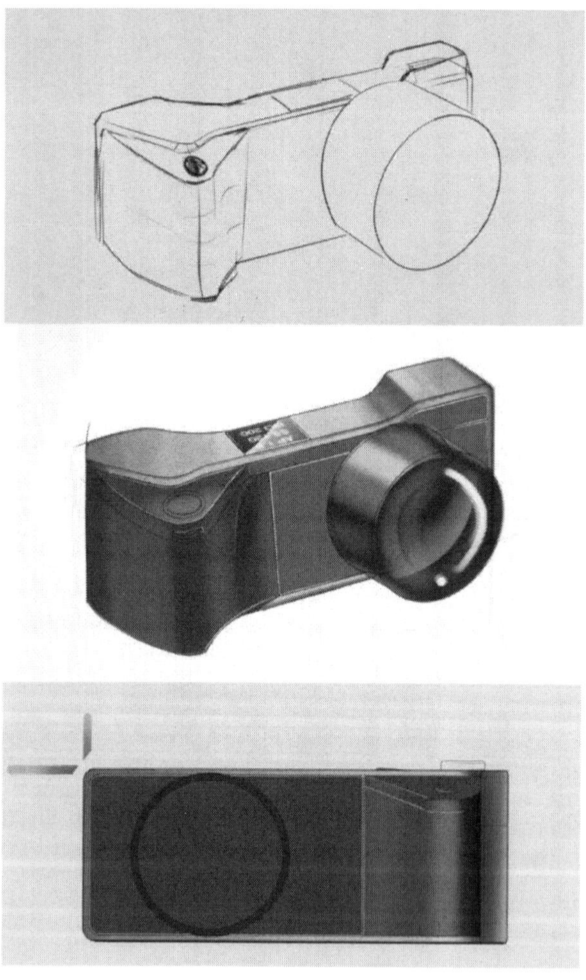

Figure 19. Concept Sketches for ControlNet 2

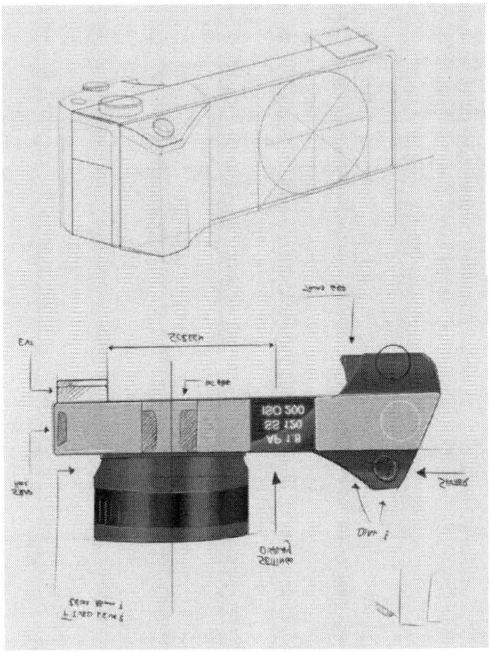

Figure 20. Selected AI generations, Evaluate 2

Refine

Then these ideas were given to Boid, and the finished concept was decided upon with the help of their industrial designer. To do this, design pieces from the generated images were chosen and put together. Figure 21 and 22 show the designed and chosen ideas and inspirations. Then, these were put together with the shape and form factor that were chosen in Evaluate 2. It was decided that this idea would be improved and made real in CAD instead of with a finished sketch. The form and comfort of the idea were also tested with 3D prints, which can be seen in Figure 23.

Figure 21. Refine Chosen Elements

Figure 22. Refine Chosen Elements 2

Figure 23. Refine Ergonomic Evaluation Prints

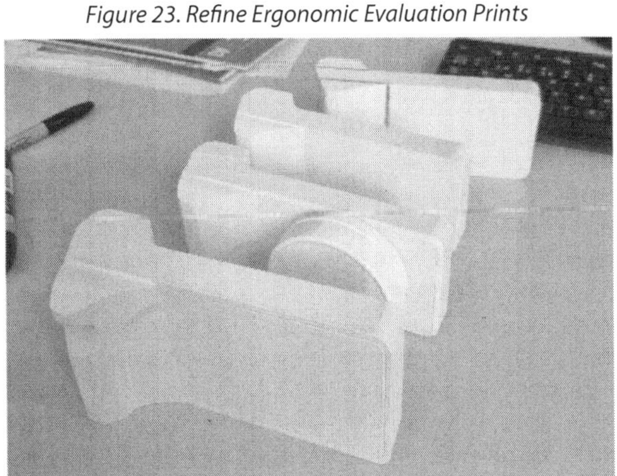

Clarify

Based on the design elements and functions that were chosen with Boid's help and the information gathered from the ergonomic tests and confirmation, work began on making a 3D model of a concept camera in CAD. Rhino 7 was picked as the tool for this step in the process, and figure 24 shows the final model of the idea.

Figure 24. Concept CAD Model

Figure 25. Final Render 1

Figure 26. Final Render 2

Figure 27. Final Render 3

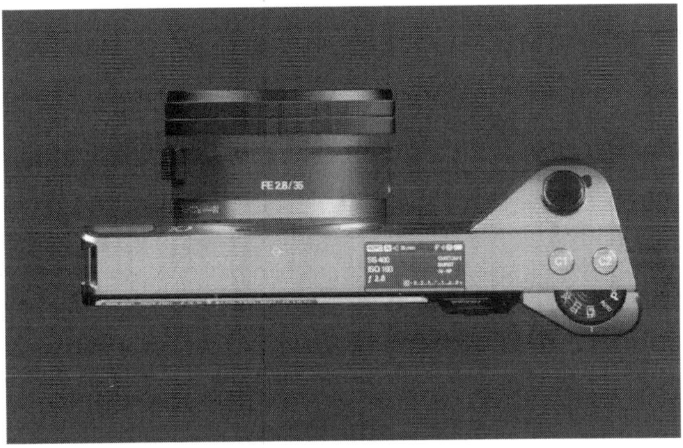

Figure 28. Final Render 4

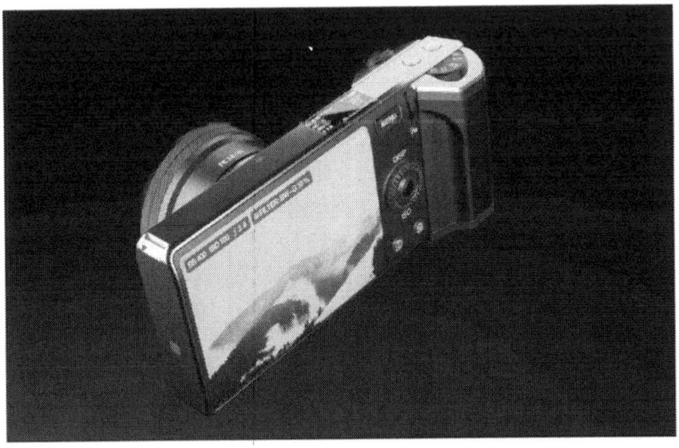

Figure 29. Final Render 5

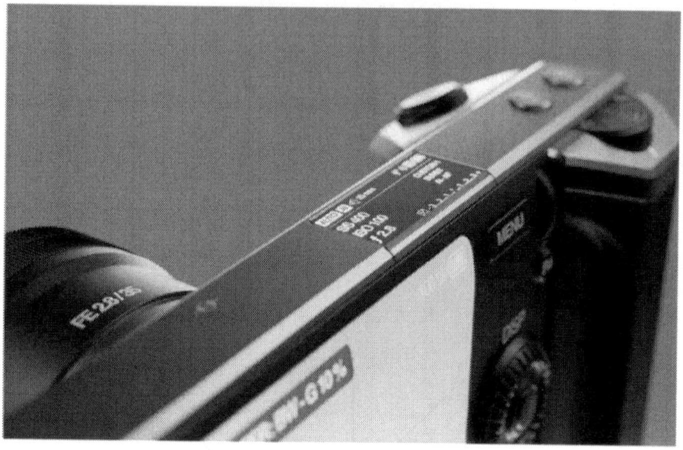

Conclusion and Discussion

Further Process Development

It is important to note that the methods developed for this thesis are only concerned with the tools that were chosen. They do not take into account any other changes that occurred during the project. Generative artificial intelligence is an area that is growing and changing quickly. As this project has gone on, more and more possible tools have come up that haven't been thought of yet. At the time of writing, the release of ChatGPT 4 and the updated Midjourney 4 is a good example. They both have amazing picture generation features with higher levels of accuracy and detail than the Stable Diffusion model used in this thesis. This was known from the start to be a risk of the thesis. It also means that the methods used here will need to be changed and updated in the future as better tools come out.

The process has also only been tried in a very short amount of time because of the thesis's time limits. This means that it has not been tested on a fully realistic project that could take months or even years to complete. In this trial, a lot less time is spent on each step, so the full results of the process cannot be fully assessed. This time, the steps that would benefit most from more time are the Define and Clarify stages. To make sure the proposed process is completely valid, it needs to be tested in a full project where enough time is available to fully carry out each step.

One possible problem with the process is that it depends on the creator having a good understanding of how to make prompts. This is because the results of the prompt and the steps that follow depend a lot on how relevant and good the images that are made are. The sheer number of pictures that are made is another problem that could come up because of generated images. There were just over 3000 images made for the planning process during the course of this thesis. Even with special tools, keeping track of all these images could be hard on bigger and longer jobs.

Further Product Development

The object that was made as part of testing the process in this thesis is only an idea. In other words, it would need a lot more work before it could be sold. The idea has been thought through in terms of how it works and how it fits people's bodies, but it doesn't take into account the problems that come up when making it or how much it would cost.

Ethics and Artificial Intelligence

As I worked on this study, I learned more about AI tools and the problems that are happening with them right now. Lack of openness is a clear problem with the way AI models work now. When an AI model is trained, you can't see the data that was used. The same is true here. I have no plans to make any money off of the model I made for this thesis, but the way the data used to train it could be seen as unethical. I think it would be unethical to try to make money off of AI models since all of the materials used in the thesis were gathered without the makers' permission.

This doesn't stop other people in the AI space from doing it, though, because there is nothing formally stopping them. This makes me wonder what will happen to images made by AI in the future. Only time will tell how society and the law change to adapt to the growth of AI tools.

I think we should learn more about how AI tools affect people's imagination as well. AI can make an infinite number of different versions of a design, but I don't think it can really come up with new ideas in a certain area. During the concept development phase, I sometimes felt stifled and limited by the AI because I became fixated on the images it produced, which stopped me from exploring ideas that weren't in the generated material.

Review of Goals and Research Questions

A list of goals was included in the report at the start of the process. Some or all of these goals have been met. The only goal that hasn't been talked about much is the moral issues that come up when AI tools are used in study.

What changes need to be made to the planning process so that AI can be used more effectively? This question was answered by creating a new process that makes use of the chosen AI tools. It's important to note that the process described in this report is just one answer to that question. I'm sure there are almost infinite other ways to use AI in this process that aren't covered in this report.

The second study question was, "What changes does a person need to make to an idea generated by AI in order to make it work as a product?" to which the process trial has given an answer. To sum up, it was found that AI doesn't take into account things like usefulness and ergonomics when it comes to functionality and human factors. Because of this, the human creator still has a lot of work to do on the product before it can fully become a useful product for people.

Chapter 6
Artificial intelligence-aided design: Smart Design for sustainable city development

Introduction

As computers get faster and better, new technologies like artificial intelligence (AI) open up new ways to solve problems in cities. These include the long-standing problems of protecting the environment, boosting the economy, and making sure everyone has a fair chance. A lot of researchers have been using these computer benefits to study cities, but most of their attention has been on the scientific discoveries that can help with planning and design. This is called "Science for Design." But for urban development to be sustainable, we also need to talk about how design should work as Design in Science, which is not well known. A new question that keeps coming up is how to plan and build sustainable towns using a smarter method that combines Design in Science and Science for Design?

However, the process of urban planning is often talked about in terms of two different meanings that are often given the same name. The first is the big-D "Design," which is the overall design process from defining the problem to finding a solution. The second is the small-D "design," which is a narrow design that focuses on a well-defined design job to come up with solutions. This is usually done as part of the overall design process. Both methods have their own problems and traits. One the one hand, the general design process is made up of a bunch of unorganized and bad ideas, like planning. One common problem is that the design process for answers depends on how well the problem is defined, which is something that often gets clearer during the design process. Having different parties take part makes things even more complicated. When you use the narrow design process, on the other hand, you look for a specific design problem in a well-defined design area. The main point of this process is to learn how to look more quickly and effectively.

The planning and design decision support tools that make the design process easier are mostly based on two schools of thought. The planning support systems (PSS) school uses loosely linked technique groups to help people make planning decisions. The generative design systems school uses computers to create new, efficient space designs. Both have pros and cons when it comes to using design, science, and math to help solve difficult urban sustainable design problems. They are very different in how they look at the two types of creation processes and how they use scientific tools in these processes.

PSS school is mostly about the planning and design process as a whole, as well as how different computer tools can be used to help with different parts of it. As people's ideas about how to plan changed, so did the general process in PSS. It went from system optimization to group design, and from linear and rational models to recursive and communicative models. PSS's narrow design process, on the other hand, often uses simple and restricted methods, like making scenarios based on current trends and the knowledge of planners and designers. Then, decisions are made based on using scientific information and tools to look at the effects of different scenarios. People have said that these kinds of post-design evaluation methods can't really help with solving hard design problems in cities with almost infinite design spaces because there are so many variables and rules. This means that the answers are often not the best ones. People in this school think that the Geodesign method is the newest model. It "tightly couples the creation of design proposals with impact simulations influenced by geographic contexts, system thinking, and digital technology." Geodesign makes the general design process more complicated, but it mostly follows the PSS school's practice of keeping things simple when it comes to the narrow design process. In this kind of setting, the suggested and chosen design options are generally not the best, since manual design and evaluation after design are common in the impact model.

Building and engineering design led to the other school of generative design tools. More attention is paid to showing real shapes and using computers to help with the narrow design process. The performance-based generative design method is a new idea that lets you search the design space in a more organized way using scientific models of performance and optimization algorithms. But most studies in the school of generative design treat the broad design process the same as the narrow design process, which has a clear problem to solve and a logical way to do it. There isn't much involvement or coevolution of design problems and solutions. From the designers' point of view, a typical generative design model sees the design development process as logical and usually linear. Another problem that comes up when generative patterns are used in cities is the issue of scale. To handle the growing complexity that comes with urban form scaling up, new ways need to be found to describe urban forms and simulate how they work at the urban scale. To solve this kind of problem, you need to look at how the space form, social activity, and support system all interact with each other.

The planning and design support systems in both schools are much better now thanks to advances in computers, especially AI research that tries to understand, create, and build cognitive systems. But the two schools still have the major problems we talked about above. A lot of people are interested in planning and designing with AI. The history of these topics is almost as long as the history of AI itself, with people trying to guess how planning and designing work and making computers that could help. Some projects that focused on narrow design generation were successful. However, early attempts to automate the general design process without recognizing how bad it is caused problems and negative outcomes, and the concept of designing with AI was called into question. In the past few years, improvements in technology, computing power, and data availability have made AI popular again. The use of AI in design (AIAD), which began in generative design, has also grown in favor. The new generation of AIAD uses goal-oriented optimization algorithms to create cities, but the structure hasn't changed, so they have the same pros and cons as the generative design school.

How can we get around the problems with the two schools described above in this new age of AI? How can we better combine design, science, and computation to help us plan and design for sustainable city growth? What part can AI play in this? The goal of this chapter is to find answers to these questions by creating a new Smart Design system that uses AIAD to make design decisions better. In this case, AI is only used for the narrow process of design generation. Designers are still in charge of the overall design process. With all the talk about AI these days, there are growing worries and fears about general AI that could replace most human workers. Some jobs that require doing the same thing over and over will be taken over by AI, but research into AI and the way humans think suggests that many of these fears are overblown or even false. Serial processors are what computers use today. They are good at both logic and serial processing. When AI is created on computers, it can do more specific and logical tasks than humans, like narrow design generation. But it's not as good at more general cognitive tasks that involve conversation, like the general design process. To get to a universal AI that can be used for general design, neuroscience needs to make big steps forward to shed light on how those mental processes work, which could take a very long time. In Smart Design, AI is not directly used in the general design process. However, AI methods can greatly assist in the creation of narrow designs.

Smart Design framework

Parts of the smart design system that are closely linked are the processes and the people who take part (see Figure 1). There are two levels of design methods in the processes section. The first level is the general design process, in which people and computers work together to help design problems and solutions evolve at the same time. The second level is the narrow design generation, in which computers and AI techniques like search algorithms are used to help with clearly defined design problems. At the first level, the Smart Design framework sees urban design as processes that create new patterns and change over time in systems that include social, environmental, technical, and built environments. This general design process is broken up into four main steps: defining the human problem, designing the interface between the human and the system, optimizing the system, and interacting between the human and the system. The second level is the stage for human-system contact and system optimization. At this level, a specific design task is briefly set up with a design goal and a schema. Advanced AI search methods are then used to solve the task. The Smart Design framework organizes the two levels of design in a way that makes system optimization and human knowledge and judgment work together to make design practices more efficient and effective. This is similar to what Batty (2018) said should happen with the next generation of AI development in planning and design.

In the participants section, real players are found by looking at how much they worked on the design project and how involved they were. Usually, there are four separate groups of experts: the public group, which is made up of regular people; the design group, which is made up of designers, engineers, and computer scientists; the regulation group, which is made up of government workers; and the implementation group, which is made up of developers and banks. Through the four stages, they are given the tools to use their knowledge to help with the design project and voice their worries in a way that is similar to how urban living labs work. Narrow design generation only needs to be watched over by designers and computer scientists. The general design process, on the other hand, includes talks and regular design meetings where everyone is welcome to take part. These design talks are based on the workflows of the framework and are mostly about the parts of the framework that are needed, like design goals and constraints. Each of these meetings is broken down into two parts. In the first part, people from the public, the government, designers, engineers, and other groups negotiate about how to define the design problem or whether design solutions are possible. In the second part, computer scientists are brought in to help translate and encode the consensus results into numerical elements that can be used as inputs for computers, such as objective functions and parameters. Planners and designers are in charge of setting up and running those talks.

A picture of this new Smart Design framework is shown in Figure 1, which shows the main parts of the framework. Here, we'll talk about the detailed models and people who take part in the four stages, as well as how they connect and form loops.

Figure 1. The Smart Design framework

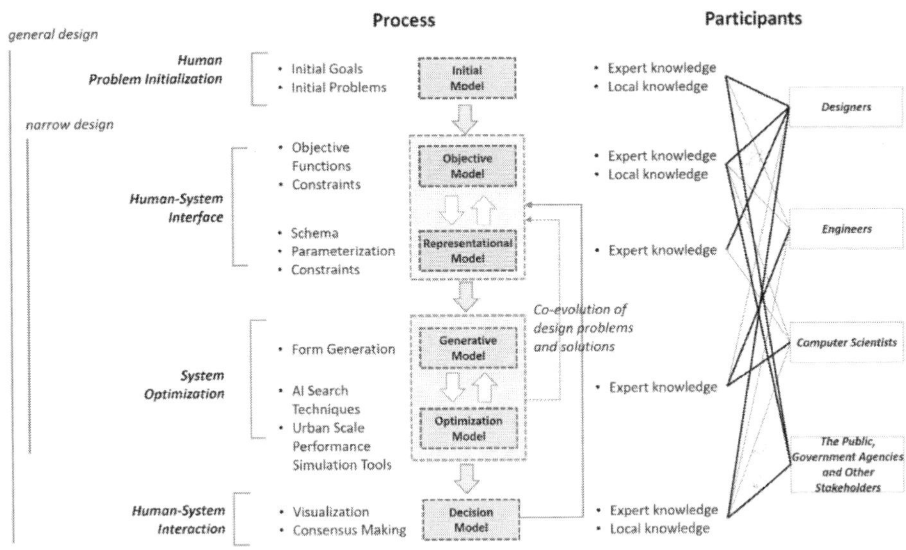

Models and Participants in Four Stages

Human problem initialization stage

The design process starts with a dilemma: it should begin with a clear problem, but the problem needs to be made clearer through study during the design process. To get out of this circle of mutual reference and start the design, the first step is to understand the design problems. In the first step of the framework, human initial problem-solving, the initial model comes up with a way to understand the problem and the goal based on a rough idea of the most important problems in the design task. When designers plan a central neighborhood, they might start by figuring out what the biggest problems are, like too much traffic and not enough public space. Most of the time, the preliminary plan isn't complete, but it can help start the process of solving the problem, and it will likely be changed and improved as the process goes on. This model puts a lot of weight on how people solve problems.

Human-system interface stage

In the second step, the human-system interface, the objective model and the representational model are used to store the explanations of the design problems in mathematical form. In the objective model, the first stage's visionary statements are looked at and turned into objective functions, such as using the least amount of energy possible. There are also restrictions found that affect the goal functions. The goal functions and constraints set the standards for judging designs, which is very important when using advanced AI search methods to look for good designs. Designers, engineers, and computer scientists need to know a lot about this model.

In the representational model, the real design of the city form is taken out and used as a starting point for later design generations. This representation has a certain structure and rules that make it fit design problems and objective functions, as well as the planned design schema that fits a certain situation and language in the given design contexts. Numerical parameterization is often used to describe how urban form is represented so that new design options can come up. The set of parameter values and the rules that govern how they relate to each other are also known as parameterization constraints. Designers and computer scientists work together to find and code the factors in this representational model, which is a big part of their job.

Both models are used to turn goals, variables, and constraints in urban design into mathematical forms. However, some of the translations are limited and depend on the designers' and computer scientists' personal views and knowledge. In later stages, human knowledge like domain knowledge and creativity will be coded to help the more advanced AI search methods.

System optimization stage

In the third stage, system optimization, the generating model and the optimization model are made. The computer programs that make design exploration possible are based on these models. It uses a parametric representation and the limits of urban form to come up with different designs when given a set of factors. The different style variations are broken down even further into geometric and semantic objects.

Advanced AI search methods, like genetic algorithms (GAs), and science performance simulation tools are used by the optimization model to help it explore the design space and find the best solutions. During the tuning process, the performance of each person or design is used to find the best fit. And science simulation tools are used to rate how well they do. A lot of different performance criteria can be used to rate the tools for sustainable urban growth. These can be economic, environmental, transportation, and visual quality performances.

In both the generative model and the optimization model, design, engineering, and computer experts play a big role in combining science modeling, design generation, and computer algorithms to find the best designs.

Human-system interaction stage

The producing model and the optimization model are made in the third stage, which is called "system optimization." Models like these are used to make the computer tools that let you explore design possible. If you give it a set of parameters and tell it the boundaries of urban form, it will come up with different designs. The different styles are split up even further into objects that are geometric and objects that are meaningful.

For example, genetic algorithms (GAs) and other advanced AI search methods are used by the optimization model to help it look through the design space and find the best answers. In the tuning process, the way each person or design works is used to find the best fit. These tools are used to rate how well they do in science. There are a lot of different ways to rate how well the tools for healthy urban growth work. There may be results related to economics, the environment, transportation, or the quality of the view.

The generative model and the optimization model both use science modeling, design generation, and computer methods to find the best designs. Design, engineering, and computer experts play a big part in both of these models.

Looping between Four Stages

This Smart Design framework is more than just a model of the four steps going in order. Instead, there are four loops inside the loop. Two of them happen again and again in the second and third steps, between the objective and representational models and between the generative and optimization models. There are two more loops that go from the third and fourth stages back to the second stage. These loops let the past definitions of the design problems and representations be changed at any point in the design process. These four loops let the design problems and solutions change together, which helps with design tasks that aren't well organized.

The framework is better than earlier support systems in the following ways. First, it focuses on design thinking and uses an iterative and recursive structure to help design problems and answers change together. Next, it combines the process of coming up with designs with scientific testing and high-tech AI search methods like genetic algorithms to help with exploring the design space. Third, it gives a way for system optimization and human understanding to work together during the design process. Fourth, it lets stakeholders be involved in the whole design process through formal steps and makes it easy for them to do so through the interfaces between figurative design and abstract computing. This lets them make better decisions based on the results of the computations.

The framework is a container that can hold different definitions of goals, constraints, methods, participants, and parametric representations so that it can be used in different settings. Because of this, it can be used for many different types of urban planning and design projects, from building new towns to redeveloping old ones.

Case study: Gangnam superblocks in Seoul

Site condition

Gangnam usually refers to the part of Seoul that is south of the Han River. The area was built up in the late 1960s, when Seoul's population started to grow very quickly. At the same time, Korea was becoming more urbanized and industrialized at a rate that had never been seen before. This fast, determined, but unprepared growth showed up as a group of superblocks, each about 800 m x 800 m and much bigger than the urban blocks you usually see in Western countries. It's important to note that each superblock has a variety of urban conditions, and the unique shape of Gangnam superblocks helps to support this diversity. In Figure 2b, you can see a figure-ground diagram of a normal Gangnam street.

Gangnam superblocks were built in three separate stages: residential buildings were built in the middle, business properties were built along the main streets inside the superblock, and high-density offices were built around the edges of the superblock. As things stand, the highest floor area ratio (FAR) that can be used in business zones is usually 8, while in residential zones it is only 3. There is no set limit on how tall a building can be, but most towers in Gangnam are less than 30 stories.

Design problems and solutions: Co-evolution in two process iterations

Gangnam is a big business hub, but its current FAR is a long way below what is allowed in the area. Gangnam's future urban rebuilding will focus on making cities denser, which will cause many environmental and energy problems, just like what's been happening in Seoul as a whole. Putting environmental goals into growth plans like the Seoul 2030 Plan could cause other problems that need to be fixed by changing the goals again.

This case study makes the densification of superblocks easier by using a made-up plan for a blank slate to show how the framework works. Even though the redevelopment will happen in small steps and change over time, having a long-term plan can help guide the process. The framework can also support the design for incremental redevelopment now that it has more knowledge on parameter ranges and constraints. Iterations of the case study are done twice. In the first round, the main goal is to maximize FAR in order to meet local needs for densification and improve economic results. The second version of the design problem takes energy efficiency into account as one of the environmental problems that comes with urbanization. This is because the first version helped the designers learn more about the design space.

The first iteration: Exploring the initial design problem

In the first round, the initial design problem is looked into by setting a starting design goal, making a rough sketch of a design schema, and choosing how to search for designs. The first goal is to maximize the FAR up to the maximum set by the zoning. The FAR limit for the whole superblock changes depending on how the superblock is designed because local planning only sets the net FAR of each parcel based on the land use. This is another example of how wicked design can be: the goal rests on the solutions. To solve this problem, a first picture was suggested that would show a stereotypical situation. The model was then updated because the design changes that came out of it included patterns that didn't work in the local setting. When the representation is changed, the optimization methods are used on this design problem and their results are compared. When answers were found, they led to talks and thoughts about the original design problem.

Representation

Gangnam superblocks' shapes can be broken down and known on different levels, such as the superblock, region, block group, block, parcel, and building levels (Figure 2 a1–a6). The formal rules come from a quick look at some old overhead photos of Gangnam that were taken in the early 1970s. They are also based on the general formal rules that Peponis et al. (2016) suggested. The official structure shows how the city has changed over time by showing how the regular and fast major street grid was built from the top down and how local streets were built from the bottom up, taking into account the city's history and culture while also making them work with modern transportation.

Figure 2. a1-a6: Structured representation of superblock; b: A figure-ground diagram of a typical Gangnam superblock

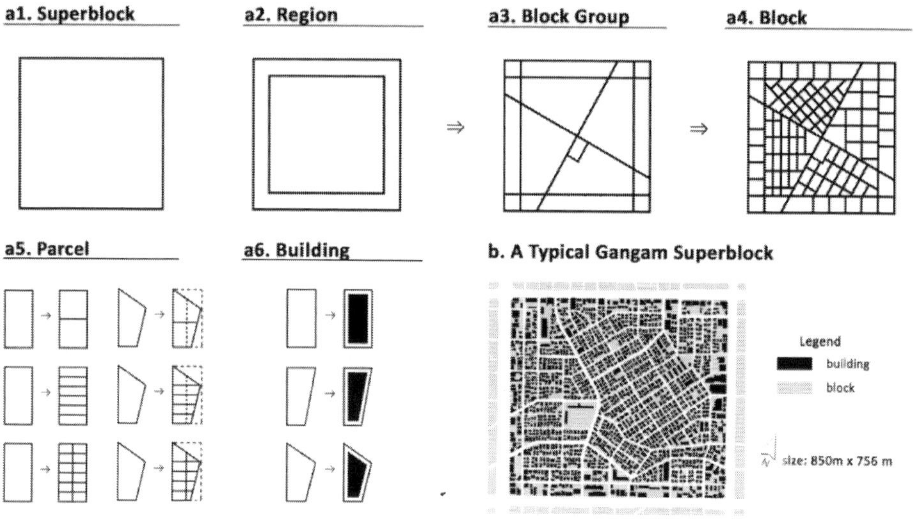

Initialization, anchor-development, peripheral blocks, interior blocks, parcels, building footprints, building envelopes, and finalization are the eight steps that made up the design schema. These steps represent the development process (Figure 2). For every step, a set of factors were used to define a sequential instance (Supplementary Table 1-2), and all of these instances together make a Gangnam superblock design.

The first step works on a scale called "region." Setting the border, peripheral ring, and interior of a superblock starts the generative process. The ring around the outside is thought to be commercial growth, and the area inside is thought to mostly be residential. The block group scale is what the second step is all about. It names an anchor block group that is angled slightly toward the middle and includes the public center. The superblock is split into 12 outer block groups, 1 center block group, and 4 inner quadrants by two streets that cross each other. The third and fourth steps work on the level of city blocks. In the third step, arrangements of blocks are set up within the outer block groups. In the fourth step, arrangements of separately oriented rectilinear grids are set up within the inner quadrants. The fifth stage works on the level of parcels. It says how pieces should be split up into blocks, which could be squares, rectangles, convex triangles, or right trapezoids. Following that, each block can be split into a 1x1, 1xn, or 2xn quad-grid layout based on its unique set of coordinates and square borders. The sixth and seventh steps work on a size of a building. In the sixth step, building footprints are defined within parcels, and setback standards are given to keep things simple. For the seventh step, building heights are set, assuming that building shells are simple prisms and that each block has a single building height. Finally, in the eighth step, the design is made as both a 3D physical model and a semantic model. There are vertices, edges, and faces in the geometric model, along with traits like land use for each geometry in the model. The semantic model has objects at different sizes.

Based on object-oriented programming, this kind of design model was then made into a class during the interface stage. Based on the numbers of 26 2D shape parameters and different height parameters, designs can be made as objects of the class.

Objective function

A superblock is usually planned as a single unit for development, and the FAR of lots inside it can be moved to give developers more options. So, the gross FAR was used to figure out how well the economy was doing. We used the zoning limits, the layout of a normal superblock, and the design schema to figure out the gross FAR limits for the outside and inside areas. These were 6.6 and 2.5, which were used as the outer and inner FAR limits. To make it more like real urban growth, a normalized one-tail FAR tolerance of 0.003 was added. The goal is to find the largest difference between two FAR values and the zoning limits, within a certain range of errors. The optimization problem is shown in Equations (1) through (3).

$$minimize: f_1(S) = D_p(S) + D_i(S) \quad (1)$$

with

$$D_p = max\left(\frac{FAR_p(S)}{6.6} - 1, 0,\ 1 - 0.003 - \frac{FAR_p(S)}{6.6}\right) \quad (2)$$

$$D_i = max\left(\frac{FAR_i(S)}{2.5} - 1, 0,\ 1 - 0.003 - \frac{FAR_i(S)}{2.5}\right) \quad (3)$$

where:

S' - design scenario defined with the design schema and parameters

D_p - function to calculate the deviation of FAR from the zoning limit in the peripheral area

D_i - function to calculate the deviation of FAR from the zoning limit in the interior area

FAR_p - function to calculate the FAR of the peripheral area

FAR_i - function to calculate the FAR of the interior area

Representation update

Based on knowledge of urban design, it was claimed that the initial design schema is too broad, leading to unrealistic urban forms. For example, buildings of impossible sizes and shapes were created, and street intersections that couldn't exist appeared. A minimum distance between street intersections, minimum areas of parcels and buildings, and minimum widths of growth parcels were all put in place to deal with this issue. The full list of design constraints that were used to update the model in this chapter can be found in Table 3 of the supporting materials.

Optimization with GAs versus stochastic enumeration

The GAs were used as the optimization method in this part. The GAs are a popular evolutionary algorithm that was based on natural selection. In GAs, each solution is described by its chromosomes, which store all of its parameters. A generation is a group of solutions. The best people from the current generation are chosen to make new people through chance crossover and mutation. This creates a new generation. This kind of iteration keeps finding answers that are close to perfect. In urban form optimization, gradient-based and brute force methods are two popular ways to find the best solution. GAs, on the other hand, are strong and reliable when the design space is big, complicated, broken up, and not well understood. A lot of engineers and architects have used this kind of method to build systems. But they aren't often used in urban planning because cities are hard to plan and don't have many performance tools for cities.

The GAs used in this chapter used a mixed-coded chromosomes model. The real-coded part has 26 general parameters, and the binary-coded part has 300 parameters for the number of floors. Choosing the operators and hyperparameters is based on comparing their success in other works. These include Deb's sorting and crossover methods, the tournament selection method, and the flipping and bounded polynomial mutation methods.

In this part, designs were made and chosen over and over again using GAs to keep the deviation from the FAR limits as low as possible. By optimizing over 60 generations with 2000 people in each generation, a total of 120,000 design variations were made and tested to find 2,351 the best design schemes that reach FAR limits (Figure 3c). Generally, the average deviation from the FAR limits decreases and the number of feasible solutions rises through generations (Figure 3 a, b). The best solutions are based on expert knowledge and local knowledge that is built into the framework. They could be workable design schemes that come from the basic superblock structure and be used for long-term growth.

The stochastic enumeration method, which makes design changes at random, was used as a comparison to see how well the optimization with GAs worked. The experiment made about 6,000,000 different random designs, but only 4 were found to be the best. Based on the comparison, it looks like the GAs were about 30,000 times more efficient at finding than the stochastic enumeration method, which is a lot better than random search.

Figure 3. The optimization results in generations using the GAs

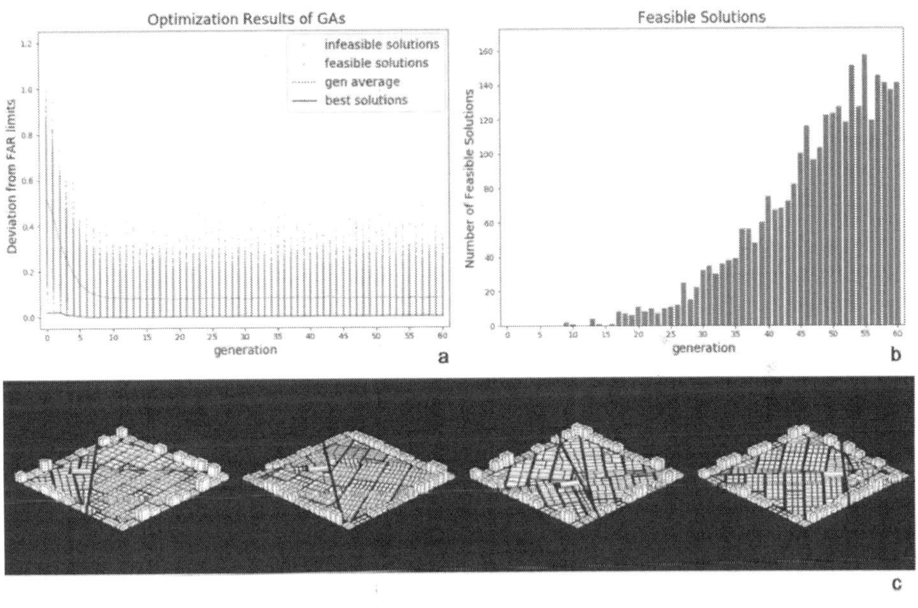

a) deviation from FAR limits; b) number of optimal designs variations; and c) axonometric projections of four generated sample designs. GAs: genetic algorithms; FAR: floor area ratio; gen: generation.

Intermediate decision-making

The best designs that were found were shown to designers so that they could include a bigger range of urban forms. Figure 3c shows a sample set of four ideas that could work. People who took part in the design process were mostly worried that making a lot of designs based on FAR goals is not nearly enough in real life. While FAR is a key goal, other goals should also be thought about in order to support long-term growth in Gangnam. The next design version was based on that problem.

The second iteration: Adding a new objective

Objective and representation updates

With the new goal of improving energy efficiency, the objective function was redefined to estimate the average building energy use intensity (EUI), and a constraint was established that the FAR of the site reaches its zoning limit. The previous objective function f_1 in the first iteration was then used in the constraint equation. The optimization problem was redefined as Equation (4) and (5).

$$minimize\text{: } f_2(S) = \frac{EU\ (S)}{A\ (S)} \tag{4}$$

subject to:

$$f_1(S) = 0 \tag{5}$$

where:

S - design scenario defined with the design schema and parameters

EU - function to calculate total building annual energy use

A - function to calculate building total floor area

The objective function f_2 was based on the urban scale building energy modeling system was developed and validated in previous studies . This system is a physically-based simulation tool to estimate building energy use at the urban scale based on the geometry and properties of buildings. It uses the EPC (energy performance coefficient) calculator as the core energy simulation engine and considers shading and microclimate effects using the Radiance and UWG developed based on TEB (Town Energy Balance) as its sub-engines . The annual energy use of each building was simulated and the average EUI of the entire superblock was calculated as the energy performance index.

The portrayal was also made better. The shape of the building, the material used, the HVAC system, how people use the building, and other factors all affect how much energy it uses. The reference building method was used for ease in the new representation. Reference buildings are building models that are common for certain types of buildings, like apartment and office buildings. They have a lot of information about the building, especially for simulating building energy use. U.S. DOE reference building dataset is one of the well-kept reference building datasets. It was made and is kept up to date by the U.S. Department of Energy based on large-scale surveys and analyses. New buildings in Seoul use the same materials and systems as those in the reference building record for New York City, but there isn't a database like this in Seoul. For that reason, the model building in New York is used as the best available data in this case study to show how buildings in Seoul use energy.

Simulation and optimization integration

For making designs, GAs and the building energy modeling tool were combined. When you combine GAs with a complex modeling system, it makes processing much harder because GAs need a lot of simulations, and each simulation takes a long time. To cut down on processing time, some strategies were used. The first was to skip the energy simulation for designs that couldn't be made because they didn't hit the FAR limits. The second step was to create an index of the designs that had already been simulated and save the modeling results so that they could be used again when the design came up in later generations. Third, make GPU parallel computing work so that all buildings in the superblock could be simulated for each plan. The fourth idea was to use distributed computing to run simulations of several plans at the same time, taking advantage of GAs' ability to work in parallel. All of these strategies cut the average time it took to simulate each design by 20 to 30 times.

With the same settings for the GAs as in the previous iteration, the optimization was run twice to prevent getting stuck early at a local optimum. In both runs, the result shows that the designs progressed toward lower EUI through the generations (Figure 4). Although the optimization paths differ, both runs reach the designs with the EUI of 298.6 kWh/m^2 after 60 generations, a significant improvement from the EUI of 327.9 kWh/m^2 and 323.6 kWh/m^2 at the beginning.

Figure 4. Optimization results from two runs: a) the first run; and b) the second run. GAs: genetic algorithms; EUI: energy use intensity; gen: generation.

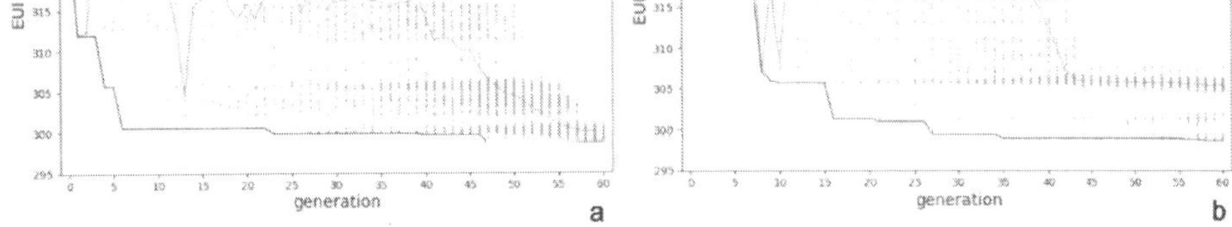

Final decision-making

As you can see in Figure 5, the optimization process went through two runs at generations 0, 20, 40, and 60. The results were shown as plans and axonometric projections. People who have an interest in the designs can better understand how they have changed over time with the help of AI programs by following the optimization process.

Figure 5. Two series of plans and axonometric projections of the designs at generations 0, 20, 40 and 60 tracing the optimization processes in: a) the first run; and b) the second run. EUI: energy use intensity; gen: generation.

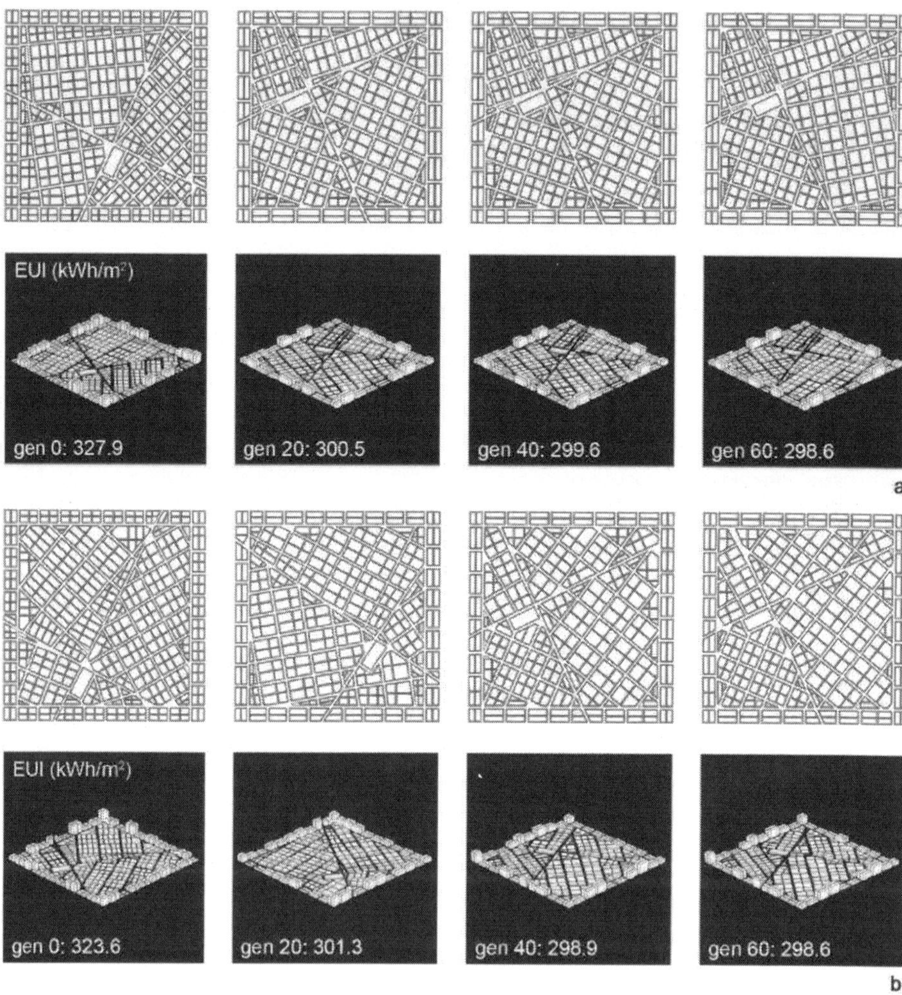

The decision model looked at and talked about the design options from the two runs. Even though both systems have the same EUI and a similar structural pattern, the details of their urban forms are different. To compare these options, we need to think about other important factors in urban planning, like how easy it is to walk, how much daylight there is, and how comfortable it is to be outside. It is likely that the design problem will need to be reframed more times to get better solutions based on feedback from people who have a stake in the project, like the people who will be using the place. This kind of revision can keep giving us better and more complete answers. However, planning time and money constraints meant that after the second round of changes, a personal choice was made between the two options. With the livability of cities as another design goal, small block size was thought of as an extra factor. This was based on Jane Jacobs' (1961) idea that big, uniform urban blocks make streets boring and dangerous. It was seen that the first design option is made up of mostly smaller buildings and has a clear linear structure, which can make the street livelier by letting small buildings open stores on their first floors. The design plan from the second run, on the other hand, has big blocks and seems too rigid. So, out of the two options, the design from the first run was chosen.

System implementation

A Python-based computing system with loose connections is used to build the Smart Design framework. An object-oriented database stores and manages the goals and models. The optimization model and the generative model are built as different modules. Python is also used to make images that help people make decisions. Parallel GPU computing and distributed computing methods have been created for this system, which makes it possible for computation times to drop by a large amount. The ways use the Accelerad and the official Python multiprocessing library in a more specific way. The distributed computing system built for this chapter used three i7 computers, and the first and second iterations took about 10 and 70 hours, respectively.

Conclusions

Planning and design are big parts of how our towns look and feel, but it can be hard to put their complicated processes into action. It just so happens that these two ideas are also important in AI study, though they have broader meanings. One thing that the studies on them in two different fields have in common is that they both want to know how to use computers to help make design decisions in certain situations. Because both fields are interested in the same thing, they can work together to solve the big problem: how to better support the design for sustainable urban growth in a complex urban environment?

To answer this big question, we need to look into two smaller ones first. The first one is how to organize and include information, knowledge, and tools from various people and sources into a formal design process that lets design problems and solutions co-evolve. Second, how can specific design scenarios be made in the narrow design generation process when design problems are already clear? In the research, the PSS focus on the first sub-question, but their answers to the second one are pretty simple and fixed. The generative design school, on the other hand, comes up with advanced ways to make limited designs, but they don't look at the whole design process as a whole; instead, they only look at it in a linear or even partial way. Both schools use scientific models and simulations to support "Science for Design," but when they talk about "Design in Science," they only talk about one of the two types of design processes.

AI researchers have also looked into these sub-questions. There are two types of AI: systems that think like humans, like knowledge-based AI for general design, and systems that think logically, like optimization systems for narrow design generation. There have been great successes in automating certain parts of the design process, but attempts to automate the whole process, like creating expert systems, have mostly failed. This is because there is an almost infinite amount of design knowledge, the cognitive system for design is very complicated, and it's hard to automate the participation from stakeholders. Even though AI is getting better, these problems are still there, even with the current wave of excitement about it. If ever made possible, a universal AI that automates the whole planning process would need a lot of progress in technology.

With the help of AI, this study created the Smart Design framework to better answer the two sub-questions and make better decisions about urban design. The Smart Design framework takes ideas from PSS's idea of complicated design processes and simplifies the overall design process as a cognitive system that combines humans and AI. The framework has four stages: initializing the human problem, integrating humans into the system, optimizing the system, and interacting between humans and the system. This kind of recursive, dynamic, and interactive structure is similar to cognitive systems in AI. However, it is built as a system that combines people and computers to handle the complexity of design, as seen in Design in Science. A method called AIAD was used in the early stages of designing the human-system interface and optimizing the system. This method uses advanced AI search techniques that are commonly used in advanced generative design methods. With the AIAD method and scientific models and tools, it is possible to quickly find the best designs in a very large design space for sustainable growth. This is an example of Science for Design. The Smart Design framework gives the two design processes a structured way to connect so that AI can help urban designers make better decisions. The framework's parts—goals, limits, parametric representations, methods, and participants—can all be changed based on the design problems and the real-world design practice.

Gangnam superblocks in Seoul were used as a case study to show how the Smart Design framework can be used to make cities more sustainable. Two versions were shown to look at how design problems and answers change over time and to find the designs with the lowest EUIs and highest FARs so that more decisions can be made. The case study shows how the framework can be put together with specific parts for a certain design case. It also shows how the formal process in the framework can help designers and planners make smart design choices that take into account the constantly changing goals for sustainable city development.

With the new framework, planning and design can now use design, science, and AI in a new and powerful way. The framework's main parts and features—such as its iterative and participatory parts, cross-scale structured representations of urban forms, and integration of modeling tools and GAs—are meant to add to the new conversation about AI and design. There are, however, still a lot of difficult problems with the framework as it is now. For example, there are questions about how to explore and update design schemata, whether the generative model should use a symbolic or visual representation, how to speed up complex urban modeling tools for goals that change over time, how to use multiobjective optimizations, and how to deal with uncertainties during the process. These issues will be looked into in more study to come.

Figure 6. a: Steinitz's Geodesign framework (2012); b: A typical generative evolutionary design framework (Janssen, 2006).

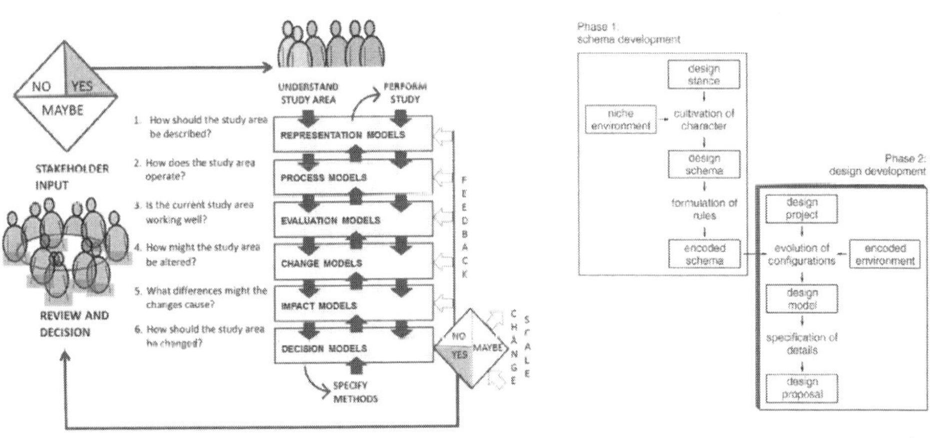

Table 1. The complete list of design constants

	Description	Spatial scale	Value
1	Superblock length	Superblock	800 m
2	Superblock width	Superblock	800 m
3	City street width	City	60 m
4	Superblock street width	Superblock	10 m
5	Building setback	Parcel	3 m
6	Peripheral block width	Block	60 m
7	Anchor block length	Block	120 m
8	Anchor block width	Block	60 m

Table 2. The complete list of design parameters

	Description	Spatial scale	Minimum	Maximum	Data type (precision)
1	Rotation angle of the axis	Region	15 °	70 °	Float (1)
2	Peripheral block length	Block group	60 m	120 m	Float (1)
3	Peripheral parcel length	Block	35 m	70 m	Float (1)
4	X of the anchor point	Region	230 m	630 m	Float (1)
5	Y of the anchor point	Region	-630 m	-230 m	Float (1)
6	Interior parcel length	Block	20 m	40 m	Float (1)
7	Translation in X of the grid for four interior block groups	Block group	-60 m	60 m	Float (1)
8	Translation in Y of the grid for four interior block groups	Block group	-60 m	60 m	Float (1)
9	Rotation of the grid for four interior block groups	Block group	0 °	75 °	Float (1)
10	Block length of the grid for four interior block groups	Block group	60 m	120 m	Float (1)
11	Block width of the grid for four interior block groups	Block group	60 m	120 m	Float (1)
12	Numbers of floors of buildings on 60 peripheral blocks	Block	1	32	Integer
13	Numbers of floors of buildings on 240 interior blocks	Block	1	8	Integer

Table 3. The complete list of design constraints.

	Description	Spatial scale	Specification
1	Distance from a superblock street intersection to a city street intersection	Superblock	>= 30 m
2	Grid generation ratio for peripheral blocks and parcels	Block; Parcel	>= 0.6
3	Peripheral extended block area	Block	>= 300 m2
4	Peripheral block area	Block	>= 300 m2
5	Peripheral parcel area	Parcel	>= 300 m2
6	Peripheral building footprint area	Building	>= 200 m2
7	Peripheral parcel width	Parcel	>= 20 m
8	Grid generation ratio for interior blocks and parcels	Block; Parcel	>= 0.6
9	Interior extended block area	Block	>= 300 m2
10	Interior block area	Block	>= 300 m2
11	Interior parcel area	Parcel	>= 150 m2
12	Interior building footprint area	Building	>= 50 m2
13	Interior parcel width	Parcel	>= 15 m

References

Alonso L, Zhang YR, Grignard A, et al. (2018) CityScope: a data-driven interactive simulation tool for urban design. Use case Volpe. International Conference on Complex Systems. Cambridge, MA, USA: Springer, 253-261. Batty M. (2003) Planning support systems: techniques that are driving planning. In: Geertman S and Stillwell J (eds) Planning Support Systems in Practice. Heidelberg: Springer, v-viii.

Batty M. (2013a) Defining geodesign (= GIS plus design ?). Environment and Planning B-Planning & Design 40(1): 1-2.

Batty M. (2013b) The new science of cities, Cambridge, MA: The MIT Press.

Batty M. (2018) Artificial intelligence and smart cities. Environment and Planning B: Urban Analytics and City Science 45(1): 3-6.

Batty M and Yeh T. (1991) The promise of expert systems for urban planning. Computers, Environment and Urban Systems 15(3): 101-108.

Buchanan R. (1992) Wicked problems in design thinking. Design issues 8(2): 5-21.

Bueno B, Norford L, Hidalgo J, et al. (2013) The urban weather generator. Journal of Building Performance Simulation 6(4): 269-281.

Bulkeley H, Coenen L, Frantzeskaki N, et al. (2016) Urban living labs: governing urban sustainability transitions. Current Opinion in Environmental Sustainability 22: 13-17.

Campbell S. (1996) Green cities, growing cities, just cities? Urban planning and the contradictions of sustainable development. Journal of the American Planning Association 62(3): 296-312.

Chase SC. (2005) Generative design tools for novice designers: Issues for selection. Automation in Construction 14(6): 689-698.

Colgan L, Spence R and Rankin P. (1991) Steering automated design. In: Gero JS (ed) Artificial Intelligence in Design '91. Oxford: Butterworth-Heinemann, 211-230.

Deb K. (2000) An efficient constraint handling method for genetic algorithms. Computer Methods in Applied Mechanics and Engineering 186(2-4): 311-338.

Deb K and Goyal M. (1996) A combined genetic adaptive search (GeneAS) for engineering design. Computer Science and informatics 26: 30-45.

Geertman S, Ferreira J, Goodspeed R, et al. (2015) Introduction to 'planning support systems and smart cities'. In: Geertman S, Ferreira Jr J, Goodspeed R, et al. (eds) Planning support systems and smart cities. Cham: Springer, 1-17.

Gen M and Cheng R. (2000) Genetic algorithms and engineering optimization, New York: John Wiley & Sons. Gero JS. (1991) Artificial intelligence in design'91: Butterworth-Heinemann.

Goel AK and Davies J. (2011) Artificial Intelligence. In: Sternberg RJ and Kaufman SB (eds) The Cambridge handbook of intelligence. Cambridge University Press.

Goodchild MF. (2010) Towards Geodesign: Repurposing Cartography and GIS? Cartographic Perspectives 66. Graham S and Marvin S. (2002) Splintering urbanism: networked infrastructures, technological mobilities and the urban condition: Routledge.

Herrera F, Lozano M and Verdegay JL. (1998) Tackling real-coded genetic algorithms: Operators and tools for behavioural analysis. Artificial Intelligence Review 12(4): 265-319.

Holland JH. (1992) Genetic algorithms. Scientific American 267(1): 66-73.

Hopkins LD. (1999) Structure of a planning support system for urban development. Environment and Planning B-Planning & Design 26(3): 333-343.

Jacobs J. (1961) The death and life of great American cities: Random House LLC.

Janssen P. (2006) A generative evolutionary design method. Digital Creativity 17(01): 49-63.

Jones NL and Reinhart CF. (2017) Experimental validation of ray tracing as a means of image-based visual discomfort prediction. Building and Environment 113: 131-150.

Kim K-J and Choe S-C. (2011) In search of sustainable urban form for Seoul. In: Sorensen A and Okata J (eds) Megacities. Tokyo: Springer, 43-65.

Klosterman RE. (1997) Planning support systems: A new perspective on computer-aided planning. Journal of Planning Education and Research 17(1): 45-54.

Knight T and Stiny G. (2001) Classical and non-classical computation. Arq: architectural research quarterly 5(4): 355-372.

Krish S. (2011) A practical generative design method. Computer-Aided Design 43(1): 88-100.

Lee S-H, Zhao F and Augenbroe G. (2013) The use of normative energy calculation beyond building performance rating. Journal of Building Performance Simulation 6(4): 282-292.

Li T, Shao G, Zuo W, et al. (2017) Genetic algorithm for building optimization: State-of-the-art survey. 9th International Conference on Machine Learning and Computing. Singapore, Singapore, 205-210.

Lynch K. (1981) Good city form, Cambridge: MIT Press.

Martins TAL, Adolphe L and Bastos LEG. (2014) From solar constraints to urban design opportunities: Optimization of built form typologies in a Brazilian tropical city. Energy and Buildings 76: 43-56.

Niitamo V-P, Kulkki S, Eriksson M, et al. (2006) State-of-the-art and good practice in the field of living labs. 2006 IEEE International Technology Management Conference (ICE). IEEE, 1-8.

Oxman R. (2006) Theory and design in the first digital age. Design studies 27(3): 229-265.

Oxman R. (2008) Performance-based design: Current practices and research issues. International Journal of Architectural Computing 6(1): 1-17.

Oxman R. (2009) Performative design: a performance-based model of digital architectural design. Environment and Planning B-Planning & Design 36(6): 1026-1037.

Peponis J, Park J and Feng C. (2016) The city as interface of scales: Gangnam urbanism. In: Kim S-H, Cinn E, Ahn K, et al. (eds) The FAR game: Constraints sparking creativity. Seoul: SPACE Books, 102-111.

Quan SJ, Li Q, Augenbroe G, et al. (2015) Urban data and building energy modeling: A GIS-based urban building energy modeling system using the urban-EPC engine. In: Geertman S, Ferreira J, Goodspeed R, et al. (eds) Planning Support Systems and Smart Cities. Cham: Springer, 447-469.

Quan SJ, Minter JD and Yang PP-J. (2013) A GIS-Based Performance Metrics for Designing a Low Energy Urban Agriculture System. In: Geertman S, Toppen F and Stillwell J (eds) Planning Support Systems for Sustainable Urban Development Heidelberg: Springer, 225-247.

Ratti C, Baker N and Steemers K. (2005) Energy consumption and urban texture. Energy and Buildings 37(7): 762776.

Rittel HWJ and Webber MM. (1973) Dilemmas in a general theory of planning. Policy Sciences 4(2): 155-169. Rowe P. (1987) Design Thinking, Cambridge, MA: MIT Press.

Russell SJ and Norvig P. (2016) Artificial intelligence: a modern approach: Malaysia; Pearson Education Limited. Schuler N, Cajot S, Peter M, et al. (2017) The optimum is not the goal: Capturing the decision space for the planning of new neighborhoods. Frontiers in Built Environment 3: 76.

Seoul Metropolitan Government. (2016) Seoul urban planning. Report, Seoul Metropolitan Government, Republic of Korea.

Seoul Metropolitan Government. (2018) Seoul Metropolitan Government Ordinance on Urban Planning. Ordinance, Seoul Metropolitan Government, Republic of Korea.

Shea K, Aish R and Gourtovaia M. (2005) Towards integrated performance-driven generative design tools. Automation in Construction 14(2): 253-264.

Simon HA. (1969) The sciences of the artificial, Cambridge: MIT Press.

Steinitz C. (2012) A framework for Geodesign: Changing geography by design, Redlands: Esri Press. US Department of Energy. (2011) Commercial Reference Buildings. Report, US Department of Energy, USA. Vonk G, Geertman S and Schot P. (2007) A SWOT analysis of planning support systems. Environment and Planning A 39(7): 1699-1714.

Ward GJ. (1994) The RADIANCE lighting simulation and rendering system. 21st International Conference on Computer Graphics and Interactive Techniques. Orlando, USA, 459-472.

Yuh O-K and Ahn K-H. (2006) A study on the development and growth of YoungDong new town. Journal of the Korean Regional Development Association 18(4): 161-182.

Index